What others are saying about this book:

A famous proverb states, "Give a man a fish, feed him for a day; teach him how to fish, feed him for a lifetime. The information in this book will teach you how to solve many of your internal problems on your own — For a Lifetime! *Christopher P. Neck, Ph.D., Department of Management Virginia Tech, Blacksburg, VA*

Dr. Durlacher has written an impressive text that is lucid, simple and orderly. In Freedom From Fear Forever, Dr. Durlacher explains vividly his techniques of Acu-POWER. The chapter on psychological reversal alone is worth the price of the book. *Edward C. Sullivan, D.C., Ph.D. Vice President, Council on Behavioral Health of the American Chiropractic Association*

I have found your book Freedom From Fear Forever of great interest and full of invaluable information. This is a self-help book that really can help and make a difference for anyone who reads it. *Evelyn Budd-Michaels, Ph.D. Reseda, CA*

I have seen the lives of my patients dramatically changed as a result of these techniques. Dr. Durlacher has done an excellent job of organizing information from a variety of sources for presentation in a very readable format. This book can change your life and the lives of your friends and loved ones. I highly recommend this book! *James D.W. Hogg, D.C., Rock Island, IL.*

An excellent volume. Dr. Durlacher has taken the best of his experience under applied kinesiology and Dr. Callahan's work and produced a book of great value to all. *George J. Goodheart, D.C. Discoverer and Developer of Applied Kinesiology, Grosse Pointe Woods, MI*

Freedom From Fear Forever

A way to eliminate your fears, phobias and inner problems.

Freedom From Fear Forever

The Acu-POWER way to overcoming your fears, phobias and inner problems.

Techniques that will help you live a life free from the fears and phobias that steal the enjoyment from your daily activities.

Dr. James V. Durlacher

Library of Congress Catalog Card 94-062181

ISBN: 0-9645713-1-5

First Edition 1995

Printed in the United States of America

Acknowledgements

There are very few really original thoughts. Most are additions or variations on the original. I want to thank Roger J. Callahan, Ph.D., a clinical psychologist who developed the original concepts and unselfishly shared his Callahan Techniques with me and the members of the International College of Applied Kinesiology as well as his own profession, from which I have utilized and added to in writing this book.

I want to thank George J. Goodheart, D.C. my mentor, for sharing his discovery of applied kinesiology, not only with me but with doctors of all disciplines.

I want to thank James A. Revels, Jr., D.C. who encouraged a thirty two year old man who "knew not what he knew" to think of how something could be done rather than make excuses. This 'something' was my enrollment in the Palmer College of Chiropractic.

I want to thank W.H. Quigley, D.C. for helping me see the importance of the emotional side of the health triangle during my college years.

I want to thank Guy McGill for his meticulous editing and suggestions to make the book more reader friendly.

I want to thank Debra Caldwell for her help in developing a title for this book.

I want to thank Barbara Read for being my photographic model.

Without patients to teach me, I certainly would not have developed some of the finer tuning of Acu-POWER. I appreciate and thank them.

I want to thank Mindy Coffman for the original concept from which the cover art work was illustrated.

Most of all, I want to thank my wife, Jackie, for not complaining about being a writers 'widow' during the many long hours I spent in the computer room and for her help in transcribing the final edit with suggestions on clarifying what I wanted to say.

Publisher's Note

Even though many people have been assisted to date by Acu-POWER procedures, there is no guarantee intended or implied, that diagnosis and treatment procedures described in this book will be effective in any specific instance.

In the vast number of people treated, the author has not found any evidence that this procedure is harmful to anyone. However, as with all new treatment procedures, you must use those described at your own risk.

If you are concerned or doubtful about the application of any of the procedures, you may want to discuss your concern with your physician, psychotherapist or religious counsel before beginning treatment.

In some instances what may seem to be any of the various problems described in this book may be a psychological problem that requires long term psychotherapy and or medication. The aid of a psychological counselor or physician should be procured.

If you are presently taking any medication for anxiety, depression or any other psychological problem, you are advised to consult your physician before stopping or reducing your medication.

The author and the publisher shall not assume any liability or responsibility, whatsoever, to any person or entity for guaranteeing that any of the conditions mentioned in the title or body of the book will be treated effectively.

To my wife Jackie, our combined children - Les, Patricia, Jo Ann, Jim, Dan, Diane and our grand children, Jason, Sonni, Schyular, Jim, John and Jake.

CONTENTS

Foreword

In 1981 two papers of mine were published in the Collected Papers of the International College of Applied Kinesiology: "A Rapid Treatment for Phobias" and "Psychological Reversal." These two papers described my findings of the previous two years (1979 and 1980) in which I found that Applied Kinesiology was a field with important potential implications for **my** field of clinical psychology. Indeed, since that time I believe that through this work we can say that the body's little known but quite well established energy system is actually the control system for **all** the negative emotions.

Dr. Durlacher was one of the AK chiropractors who immediately took a special interest in my psychological finding. As he states, his long term interest in the nature and role of psychological problems led him quite naturally to explore the implications of my discoveries.

This book is a contribution to the treatment of fears and phobias and it is especially valued because of the solid background in chiropractic and applied kinesiology which Dr. Durlacher brings to this work.

To my knowledge, Dr. Durlacher is the only other doctor, at this point, besides myself, who has actually treated people with phobias on live television. The reason I mention this is that one has to have some confidence in the effectiveness of the procedure in order to undertake this highly public and professionally vulnerable task. Even with confidence, of course, one may fail in this or any other setting. Lest one assume that treating clients, especially skeptical strangers, of their phobias in as public a situation as is television, is an easy task, let me assure them that it is not.

The poor volunteer is made more nervous by the awareness that it is likely that a very feared object or situation will be encountered.

Added to this is the fact that one with a phobia has little or no hope (based on past experience) of being free of the intense fear; they look stupid and cowardly to the numerous viewers. Many people with phobias are unfortunately ashamed. It is understandable but is due to the mistaken idea that phobias represent a moral weakness. (Actually, my conviction is that the majority of phobias are fundamentally inherited.) Adding to all these stressful considerations for the courageous person with a phobia who volunteers to be on a live television show, is the fact that most people suffer from an additional intense phobia for appearing in front of an audience and on camera. As you may now realize, it is not easy to treat people with phobias on television. I congratulate Dr. Durlacher for courageously taking on the difficult and important task of demonstrating these procedures on live television. (Public demonstrations are important in order to show the power and ease of these treatments, which of course, are difficult to believe.)

Lastly, it is important that the interpretations of the treatments in Dr. Durlacher's book reflect his own development of ideas about phobias apart from mine. In fact, there are some notions, especially the role of beliefs and cognition in psychological problems, that are radically different from my own.

It is my conviction that these treatments cannot be adequately interpreted by conventional psychological theory but require a revolutionary theory.

Theory, of course, is of little import to a person with a phobia; what is important is to be rid of the phobia and this book shows how it can be done with a high degree of success. In science, it is desirable to have differences and competing ideas which can be experimentally tested. But regardless of theory differences, the inescapable empirical fact remains - the treatments contained herein are probably the most powerful

treatments for phobias in existance, and Dr. Durlacher's book
will help spread the word and the knowledge.

Roger J. Callahan, Ph.D.
Indian Wells, California

Introduction

Many people know more about the moon which is 250,000 miles from earth than they do about themselves. This lack of knowledge is the result of the fact that most people seem to try to find out about themselves by looking around rather than at and within themselves.

There is a story about God and three angels in which God says to the angels, "Where shall we hide the secret of life? "One angel replies by proposing that it should be buried in the depths of the ocean but God said, "No, with modern technology it would be found fairly fast." The next angel proposed that it should be hidden on the highest mountain, to which God replies, "No, where there is a mountain, it will be climbed and explored and the secret will be found." The third angel said, "I know, let's hide the secret of life inside each individual." And God replied, "I think you've got it, no one will think of looking there!"

In this book you will be able to look into your own body, your body's nervous system, where all things that have happened to you from the time of conception are recorded. Through the use of the procedures that you will learn, you will be able to literally ask if the body has any phobias, fears, anxieties, addictions, compulsive behaviors, negative life beliefs, unresolved issues or evidence of post traumatic stress syndrome. In addition, it will teach you to treat and in most cases abolish these things without the use of drugs or long drawn out counseling sessions so you will be free at last. The new method is done by stimulating certain acupuncture points on the body -- tapping on them with your fingers. This has the same effect as inserting an acupuncture needle without being invasive. The tapping procedure can take as little as five minutes in very simple cases or hours over the course of a number of sessions if there is a very complex problem. Usually, however, most problems are overcome in less than fifteen minutes.

Use the information you find in this book. Free yourself, your loved ones, your friends, or your patients of the self-defeating behaviors that have kept you or them prisoners with the use of Acu-POWER.

Whether lay person or professional, you can use the Acu-POWER procedures in this book so that:

> phobias
> anxieties
> addictions
> love pain
> rejection
> post traumatic stress syndrome
> compulsive behavior
> self-limiting and
> self-destructive   negative life beliefs

will no longer rule your life or the lives of your loved ones and or individuals you treat.

This book is written in layman's language that everyone can understand. It teaches you step-by-step how to conquer and eliminate even life long phobias with a rapid, effective method which was originally pioneered by clinical psychologist, Roger J. Callahan, Ph.D.. I call it Acu-POWER. This method does not require any 'talk-out' sessions or getting 'deep insight' into the origins of the problem. In fact, it is not necessary to reveal the phobia or any painful or embarrassing events. Your body knows exactly what is bothering it and how to correct it.

One in nine people have a significant phobia which affects how they live their lives. Almost everyone has a phobia of some kind. Many of these individuals do not realize they have a phobia, but will say, "I just don't like to be in crowds" or "I feel nervous when meeting new people" or "I'd rather drive because I enjoy the scenery".

Acu-POWER will enable you to be free at last.

Chapter 1

Your Body Knows

Everything that has ever happened to you is recorded in your nervous system -- everything. From the moment of conception, to your birth and up to today, every change in the physical, chemical and emotional condition of your mother which had an effect on you, positively or negatively, is recorded. Any trauma that occurred during your birth is recorded. Everything that happens to you throughout your entire life is recorded. Everything that is said to you is recorded. Everything you see, hear, feel, touch, taste or smell that affects you on a physical, chemical or emotional basis is recorded in your nervous system. The way this affects you depends on how effectively your nervous system is functioning.

Fortunately, your body has a screening or filter system that neutralizes many of the adverse effects of these events, so that you are not overwhelmed with non life-threatening information. This system, when functioning normally, sorts the important information (that affecting survival) from the not-so-important information. When this system is not functioning normally, stimuli that ordinarily would not bother us are allowed to create a state of fear or anxiety because we begin to view the stimuli as life threatening, rather than just a mild disturbance. This system also acts on the life-threatening information and records survival procedures, which will help us if we encounter the same or similar events in the future. It also neutralizes the fight or flight mechanism for that event, so we are prepared to act on a new-life threatening event if necessary.

We have all known individuals who have been affected by horrendous and/or tragic events suffered by themselves or by their loved ones, and who have grown from the experiences. Conversely, we all know individuals who crumble when facing the most minor problems like spilling a cup of water or being criticized. Others are afraid of common things that would not even bother most people. Those in the latter group have a malfunction in their screening system, which predisposes them to "make mountains out of mole hills".

Most of what is recorded is not in your conscious memory but rather in your sub-conscious where it can affect you physically, chemically, or emotionally throughout your life. Dr. George J. Goodheart, Jr., a chiropractic physician and lecturer, always starts his seminars with quotations from the great humanitarian and physician, Dr. Albert Schweitzer and the renowned researcher Dr. Hans Selye. The first said, "Happiness is good health and a bad memory." The words of Dr. Hans Selye are, "God will forgive you but your nervous system will not." Goodheart explains that if you do not correct the disturbance in the nervous system, there will be adverse effects in the physical, chemical and emotional sides of the health triangle. (More on this in Chapter 4.)

There are two basic fundamentals of life -- happiness and misery (unhappiness). The dictionary defines happiness as "the state of well-being and contentment or pleasurable satisfaction." It defines misery as "a condition of great suffering, a state of emotional distress."

It would then follow that the state of real or imagined fear which makes up a phobia, produces anxieties, addictions, love pain, rejection, post traumatic stress syndrome, compulsive behavior, self-limiting and self-destructive negative life beliefs. Fear causes misery.

Fear, real or imagined, produces pain. This can be physical and/or mental. We've all heard the expression, "I just can't think (or talk) about that, it's too painful", or "thinking (or talking) about that gives me a headache."

In his book Quantum Healing, Deepak Chopra discussed the fact that the brain produces internal pain killers, endorphins and enkephalins, which every neuron in the body has the ability to produce. These natural narcotics made by the body are up to two hundred times stronger than any man made pain killers and are non-addictive. He goes on to suggest the possibility of doctors anesthetizing their patients by stimulating some regions of the brain through the use of Chinese acupuncture.

This book is not about covering up pain with natural internal pain killers, but rather balancing the subtle energies of the acupuncture system so the individual can deal with his/her fears. If the body, in the process, eliminates physical pain as well, so be it.

Gabriel Cousens, M.D., in his introduction for the book, Vibrational Medicine, by Gerber says, "...we, as human organisms, are a series of interacting multidimensional subtle-energy systems, and that if these energy systems become imbalanced there may be resulting pathological symptoms which manifest on the physical/emotional/mental/spiritual planes."

Fortunately, there is a way to diagnose and treat the fear causing these adverse states. Your body knows what is causing this misery. Remember, everything has been recorded in the nervous system.

Because your body knows exactly what the problem is and will share this secret if asked, there is a way to handle all fears. The key to understanding and treating phobias is balancing the energies in the body with a very simple stimulation of specific acupuncture points. I call this Acu-POWER. The process is simple. By manually tapping on these points for about fifteen seconds and monitoring the body's responses, you can put an end to your misery and be free at last.

Chapter 2

Applied Kinesiology - Its Discovery and Development.

> 'Whenever a new discovery is reported to the scientific world, they say first, 'It is probably not true.' Thereafter, when the truth of the new proposition has been demonstrated beyond question, they say, 'Yes, it may be true, but it is not important.' Finally, when sufficient time has elapsed to fully evidence its importance, they say, 'Yes, surely it is important, but it is no longer new.'
>
> Michel de Montaigne in the 16th century

A breakthrough in diagnoses occurred in 1964 when a Detroit chiropractic physician, Dr. George J. Goodheart, Jr., made an observation so profound that it will forever be a landmark in the history of all health care -- whether provided by medical, osteopathic, chiropractic, dental, podiatric, naturopathic, homeopathic or psychologic doctors. He noted that although a patient had a significant weakness of his right serratus anticus muscle (which is attached to the underside of the shoulder blade on one end and goes around to the side of the rib cage to insert on the ribs in front, holding the shoulder blade flat against the ribs), which prevented him from pushing his arm forward, there was no atrophy of muscle size. However, on palpation (touching and feeling a part of the body with the fingers) of the origin and insertion of the muscle, there were nodules that were quite painful.

After rubbing the nodules at the origin and insertion and retesting the muscle, Dr. Goodheart was surprised to notice an immediate strengthening. After retesting for several weeks, the muscle remained strong! His first thought was, why is that? He then began testing the muscles of other patients and noted that with certain deviations of posture that certain muscles would be weak -- not able to "lock" into a resistance state. He also observed that when a muscle was in an obvious contracture state or spasm, there was a weak antagonist. He hypothesized that the spasm occurred because the muscle had no opposition from its antagonist (the opposing muscle). The good muscle simply did its job and contracted, causing the spasm. Dr. Goodheart then reasoned that rather than treating the spasmed muscle, if the weak one were to be made strong again using the origin and insertion method, the body's normal physiology should, in theory, relax the spasmed muscle. And it did!

Being an insatiable researcher, Goodheart regularly read many medical, osteopathic and chiropractic journals and books. Chapman, an osteopath, wrote of the organ reflexes he discovered on the abdomen and back, which when stimulated by a rubbing action, released toxins from the organ through the lymphatic system. Bennett, a chiropractor, discovered reflexes on the head that when stimulated by a very light steady tugging touch, restored normal blood circulation to their respective organs.

Goodheart observed that when certain reflexes were stimulated, certain muscles would regain their strength consistently. The same reflexes strengthened the same muscles every time. In addition to the normal diagnostic procedures, he then had another way of diagnosing the function of particular organs, at least on an empirical basis.

Goodheart read the discoveries of another osteopath, W.G. Sutherland, who measured the rhythmic movements of the skull bones, Sutherland found that if certain skull bones did not move normally, there would be symptoms of disease or abnormal function in the body and corresponding weak muscles. Goodheart also found that restoring normal motion to the skull would abolish the symptoms or abnormal function. He observed that it also strengthened the corresponding weak muscle.

Goodheart next studied acupuncture and its relationship to the nervous system. He found that Asians used the word CHI (pronounced, chee) meaning "life force" to describe energy they said flowed through the various meridians of the body. Again, Dr. Goodheart found that the same muscles associated with the organs were also associated with the corresponding energy organ meridians (more on meridians and CHI in Chapter 8.)

Goodheart shared the discoveries of his continuing research with others through lectures and seminars. He was in great demand by various state and national chiropractic associations and colleges. Very soon after his initial discovery he was invited to speak to the Wayne State Medical School. Upon arriving at the lecture hall, he noticed that an unidentified medical student, having learned that Dr. Goodheart was a chiropractor, had added "????" after the title of "Dr." on the poster announcing his appearance that day. After the lecture Dr. Goodheart noted the poster again and found that the "????" had been crossed out, and "!!!!" took its place.

Soon, Goodheart found that he alone was not going to be able to keep up with the demand to learn this new science, which he has named Applied Kinesiology. He began conferring the title of "Study Group Leader" to doctors who had demonstrated proficiency and ability to teach the science to others.

As more and more doctors learned the techniques, they too added new discoveries. In 1974 one of Goodheart's Study Group Leaders, John Thie, D.C., suggested that rather than remaining a loose group of doctors, they band together and form an organization to perpetuate Goodheart's teachings and standardize the curriculum and establish criteria for new teaching doctors. There were 39 original Study Group Leaders who were named as Diplomates of the newly formed International College of Applied Kinesiology (I.C.A.K.). This author was one of them.

At first, only chiropractic physicians were allowed to join the study groups; many felt that it should stay that way. Dr. Goodheart was instrumental in convincing members of the I.C.A.K. to change the by-laws to allow any type of doctor licensed to diagnose, the opportunity to attend the college. Dr. Goodheart felt that bridges, as opposed to barriers, would lead to better understanding.

Attracted by this policy, psychiatrist John Diamond, M.D., studied applied kinesiology and became a member of I.C.A.K. He learned that Goodheart had discovered that if a patient thought of something that made him/her anxious, a previously strong muscle would "weaken". Diamond used this phenomenon in working with patients and found that he could reach the core of emotional problems far faster than by using orthodox counseling. It changed his entire practice.

Diamond was an officer of the International Academy of Preventive Medicine, which at that time refused to admit chiropractic physicians as full members. Because he felt that this was discriminatory, Dr. Diamond educated members of the board of directors, who subsequently changed their by-laws to allow chiropractic physicians to become full members. Dr. Goodheart, and many other members of the I.C.A.K., including this author, subsequently applied and were admitted as full members of the I.A.P.M.

Dr. Goodheart was a featured speaker at one of the I.A.P.M. annual conventions and introduced applied kinesiology to the attending doctors. Among them was nationally renowned psychiatrist Harvey Ross, M.D., who was very impressed with applied kinesiology -- particularly the diagnostic phenomenon of a muscle weakening when a person experienced anxiety or when he/she made a statement that was false.

On returning to Los Angeles, Ross shared what he had learned with his good friend, Roger Callahan, Ph.D. Ross demonstrated the technique, and Callahan, who was very impressed, wanted to learn more of the procedure. He contacted Dr. Goodheart and found that there was a 100 hour course beginning in Los Angeles.

In 1985 Callahan wrote a book, <u>Five Minute Phobia Cure</u>, Enterprise Publishing, Wilmington, DE., for both laymen and professionals. He states in the book, "The idea that mental attitude could so directly affect body reactions intrigued me. I investigated further and subsequently attended a course in applied kinesiology, taught by David S. Walther, D.C. and Robert Blaich, D.C., at which I was the only psychologist present. Gradually, I began to see connections that permitted me to take what I had learned and adapt it to psychological problems."

A revised edition of the book was published in 1986 and renamed, <u>How Executives Overcome Their Fear of Public Speaking and Other Phobias.</u>

Two papers Callahan wrote in 1981, after he became a member of the I.C.A.K., entitled <u>A Rapid Treatment of Phobias and Psychological Reversal</u> intrigued me. After using the procedures with much success I soon found that they had potential for treating difficult cases. After meeting Dr. Callahan for the first time in 1985, I phoned him and found him to be very generous in sharing new information and treatments.

Dr. Callahan can be reached at 45350 Vista Santa Rosa Indian Wells, CA 92210 (619) 345-9261 or for free information 800-359 C-U-R-E-

Chapter 3

Physician Heal Thyself

By the end of 1985, a very stressful year, this author, who stands a full five foot, five inches, had reached 193 pounds. My clothes didn't fit, my clinic jacket had expanded from a medium to a large and I was puffing after just one flight of stairs.

To deal with stress I used food and alcohol as my tranquilizers. The alcohol was in the form of one or two scotches or martinis before dinner. After all, I rationalized, I had worked hard all day and deserved it! I could afford it and I liked it. I also enjoyed a little wine with dinner three or four times a week, and occasionally an after dinner drink. I never got "bombed out" or had a hangover -- it was just a way I relaxed in the evening.

Because of the extra calories and the increased appetite that the alcohol produced, I gained the weight. I told myself that I should lose weight, so I decided to cut out the before dinner drinks and the wine. I would fix myself a sugarless tonic water with a twist of lime, while my wife would have her usual drink because she did not have a weight problem. All went well for a few days. I had resisted temptation but soon I found myself taking a "sip" of my wife's drink. On succeeding days, this turned into several "sips," to the point that I was "sipping" at least half of her drink! She would ask, "Why don't you just fix yourself a drink?" It was then that I realized that I couldn't go without that before dinner drink: I was, if not a full blown alcoholic at least a before dinner alcoholic. I had to do something about it.

Around that time I received information from Dr. Callahan advertising his audio tapes dealing with phobias and to my welcome surprise, weight loss. I ordered the weight loss tape and found that using the procedure, I was able to conquer my addiction for food and alcohol. In a year and a half, without any special "dieting" I lost 45 pounds. The treatment simply took away my anxiety and my desire to eat and drink compulsively.

For as long as I can remember I have had a phobia regarding anything getting too close to my eyes. Occasionally at dinner, either my wife or someone would gesture with a fork in hand and if it came within one foot of my face I would cringe with the sickening feeling that I would be poked in the eye. I also could not watch anyone put in or take out their contact lenses and certainly could not even imagine having them in my eyes. I would not allow an eye doctor to perform a glaucoma pressure test using the numbing drops to take a physical contact pressure. I did very reluctantly allow the air puff test but felt very squeamish about it. My father-in-law had cataract surgery and wanted to tell me about it but I refused to let him because I couldn't even stand the thought of it. Occasionally on the educational channel there would be a program showing an actual cataract operation. I would either leave the room, change the channel or turn it off.

This phobia was unrealistic and I knew it, but I couldn't help it. I finally decided to treat myself for the eye phobias. First, I treated myself for my inability to watch someone put in and take out their contact lenses. It took about five minutes. Then I treated myself to allow the glaucoma test and succeeded in that also. To my pleasant surprise on my next visit to the eye doctor I allowed him to do the contact glaucoma test and was very relaxed. At that time I also discovered that I was developing a cataract! I treated myself for my fear of the eye surgery, and am happy to report that I went through the surgery with no apprehension whatsoever.

Chapter 4

The Triad of Health

Health is like an equilateral triangle, its components being physical (structural), chemical (nutritional) and psychological (emotional). (See Figure 1.)

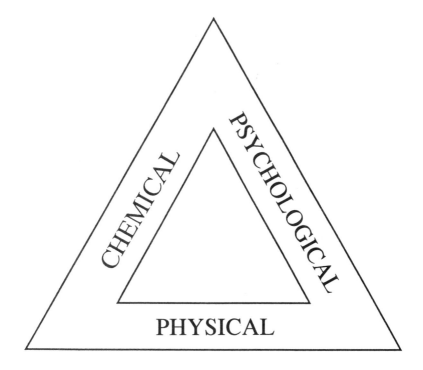

Figure 1

The triangle appears differently to various types of doctors, depending on their particular approach to health. To chiropractic physicians, orthopedists, old time osteopaths and physiatrists, it looks like Figure 2.

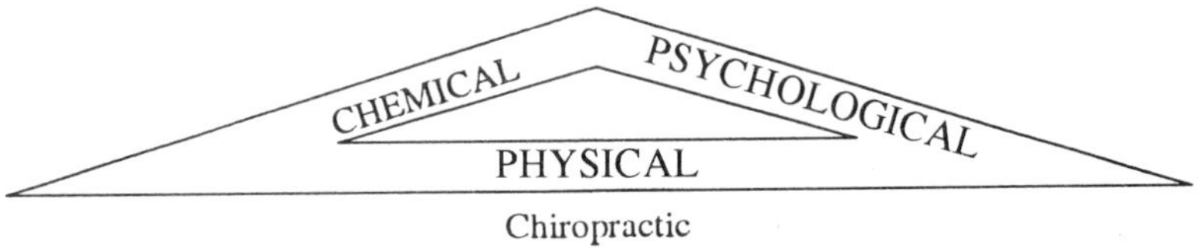

Chiropractic

Figure 2

To the allopaths (M.D.'s), homeopaths and nutritionalists it looks like Figure 3.

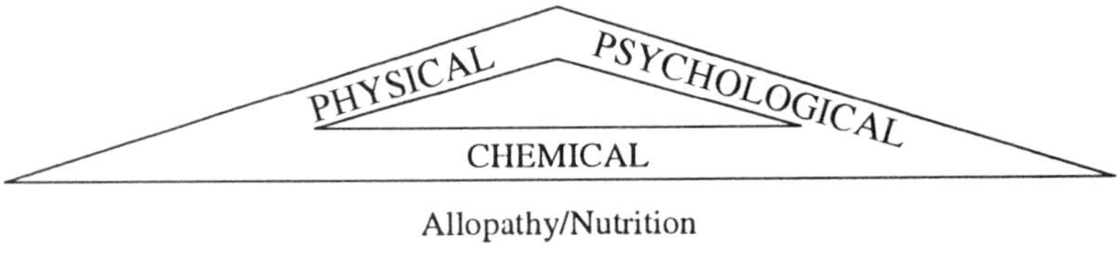

Allopathy/Nutrition

Figure 3

To the psychiatrists and the psychologists it looks like Figure 4.

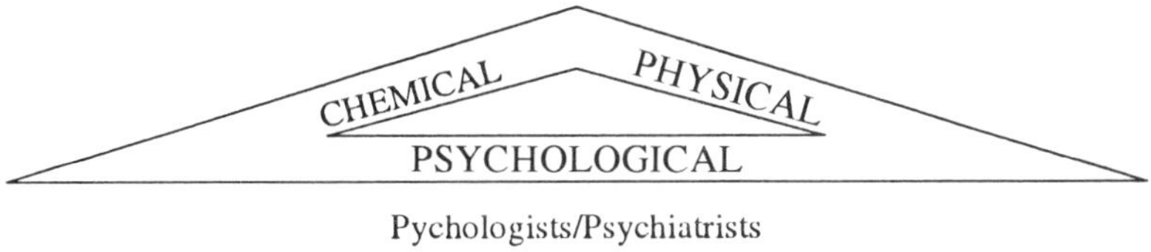

Pychologists/Psychiatrists

Figure 4

Each type of doctor places a different emphasis on what is most important. Doctors with the physical (structural) approach feel the structure is the most important aspect and that if the structure is in proper alignment everything else would follow. Doctors with the chemical (nutritional) approach feel the body could be completely regulated by chemical alterations; therefore, the chemical side is most important. And, doctors who treat psychological (emotional) conditions feel that if the patient could get his or her mind free of emotional hang-ups, that would regulate everything else.

It seems that everybody is somewhat right and also somewhat wrong. In the words of Dr. William Harper in his book by the same name, Anything Can Cause Anything.

The distortion of the structure can and does cause changes in the physiology. For instance, a person with one leg shorter than the other can have back pain. A person who has a subluxation of a vertebra with a resulting impingement of the nerve can suffer a loss of function in the muscle and/or organs which that nerve supplies. This creates, in some cases, chemical imbalances. For example, I once had a skiing injury that caused a vertebral subluxation. This impinged a nerve which led to the liver causing jaundice within a week and a significant appetite loss. It was only after the proper spinal adjustment that I returned to normal. Anything from mild to severe structural distortion, such as a scoliosis, can certainly affect someone's emotional health by making him/her constantly self-conscious of the distortion and how it appears to others. From the nineteen forties to the early sixties there was a considerable amount of clinical research done at the Clearview Sanitarium in Davenport, Iowa (owned then by the Palmer School of Chiropractic) in which a number of previously incurable mental patients were totally cured or substantially helped by chiropractic adjustments to the spine.

Changes in the chemical balance of the body caused by environmental pollutants, poor nutrition or bad hygiene can make a person physically ill and mentally ill. The ingestion of too much junk food -- processed food that lacks the proper nutrients -- can cause physical conditions such as scurvy, beriberi, pellagra, osteoporosis and bowlegedness. Ingesting too much processed food can also cause emotional conditions such as depression, hyperactivity and anxiety. Ingesting heavy metals can cause learning disorders and cancers.

And who hasn't experienced a complete loss of appetite after hearing shocking news, or blushed when they are embarrassed? It is possible to see a structural change in the posture of a person who was just divorced or fired from a job. Even without the sound on, or a look at the score after a televised sporting event, one can tell who won or lost the game by the players posture.

Again, anything can cause anything; the doctor who looks at all three sides of the health triangle, and understands that they are interrelated and interdependent, is the total-person doctor (See Figure 5).

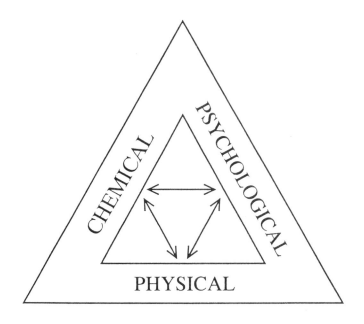

Figure 5

Of course, we need specialists. But these specialists need to look beyond their particular area of expertise and learn to recognize that other sides of the health triangle may be affecting a patient's ability to get well. This includes learning to recognize when to refer the patient, or develop the skills that will be taught in this book.

Bill Moyers interviewed Candace Pert, Ph.D., for his P.B.S. series "Healing and The Mind" (which was published in his book of the same title). Dr. Pert told of her interest in consciousness and thought. She felt that studying the brain would be fruitful. She discovered that endorphins and other chemicals like them are found not just in the brain, but in the immune system, the endocrine system, and throughout the body, and that these molecules are involved in a psychosomatic network. It turned out that these molecules are peptides, that is, they are made of amino acids, the building blocks of proteins. They are strung together, very much like a string of various colors of pearls in various lengths. She goes on to say that the peptide, enkephalin, the brain's own morphine, is only five amino acids long but others like insulin, are a couple of hundred amino acids long.

Dr. Pert found that not only the morphine peptide, but just about all the peptides in the brain were in the immune system and everywhere else! From this, she theorized that these neuropeptides and their receptors are the biochemical correlates of emotions. She concludes the interview by saying, "We'd better seriously entertain theories about the role of emotions and emotional suppression in disease, and that we'd better pay more attention to emotions with respect to health."

Many thousands of years ago, the healers of China and India found that the various energy channels -- acupuncture meridians were associated with specific emotions, and if there was a disturbance in these energy channels, there would be a disturbance in the physical and emotional well-being of the individual.

This book is intended to provide information to laymen to help themselves and to doctors to help their patients. For laymen, the skills you learn here will enable you to help yourself and your loved ones to a healthier life. Of course, referrals to mental and emotional health specialists will be necessary in some cases. For the doctor, this book will teach skills to help you be a more efficient and better doctor. It will expand your knowledge and skills, and give you tools to help diagnose and treat the mental side of the health triangle.

Chapter 5

Why Can't I Or My Patients Get Any Better? Psychological Reversal - Self-Sabotage

Why is it that some individuals either don't respond at all, or reach a certain point in their recoveries, but then stop? Why do some individuals continue to fail in life, business, sports or whatever they attempt to do, when they have the ability and potential to succeed? These are questions that many doctors ask as they treat patients, and also ask of themselves.

Psychologists and psychiatrists have long known that some patients have self-defeating natures. For these people everything they attempt seems to go wrong, or turns out to be less than they had hoped for. They resist treatment, but profess that they want to be cured. These individuals have been described as "losers" (we have all seen the comic strip, "The Born Loser"), negative personalities or self-destructive people. They have a death instinct, or exhibit self-defeating behavior. Perhaps it was best described in a comic strip "Pogo", popular in the 50's and 60's, when Pogo said, "We have met the enemy and they are us!"

Psychologists and psychiatrists are not the only type of doctors who encounter patients with these problems; most doctors probably deal with negative personalities on a regular basis. It doesn't matter whether patients suffer from physical or emotional diseases, if they have what Callahan coined as "psychological reversal" they will not respond to your best treatment efforts or techniques until the psychological reversal is corrected.

Psychological reversal is a condition in which patients say that they want to get well, but subconsciously they do not. They say that they want to do something or accomplish a particular goal, but they either subtly or grossly sabotage their own efforts and fail or don't even try. The body knows this is occurring, for if you test the strength of an individual's muscle immediately after they state they want to accomplish something, if they are psychologically reversed, they will test weak (See Chapter 6). (An exception to this is if the individual is neurologically disorganized, a topic that will be discussed thoroughly in Chapter 8.)

Psychological reversal occurs in all areas of life -- someone may be trying to regain health, educate themselves, write, compose music, succeed in business, a profession, the arts or excel in sports.

There are three major degrees of psychological reversal:

1. Massive

2. Specific

3. Mini

There is a song that was popular a few years ago performed by Bobby McFerrin and entitled, "Don't Worry, Be Happy!" This certainly is an excellent thought but suppose it is not possible to be happy? Suppose someone's energies are so mixed up that as long as this imbalance exists he/she would rather be miserable?

Massive psychological reversal is a state in which an individual is reversed on every aspect of life. If the individual makes the statement, "I want to be happy", he or she will test weak. Conversely, if the statement was made, "I want to be miserable," he or she would test strong! An individual would test weak for any positive statement made regarding his/her wants or goals, and test strong for any negative statements. These are the people who never get anywhere in life, who are termed "born losers" -- the "down and out," the homeless, the perennial welfare recipients and in more severe cases, the criminals, particularly repeat offenders and murderers.

The irony in this is that society makes fun of those individuals. I am reminded of a syndicated single panel cartoon called "Charlie" in which Charlie is standing in front of the counter of the birth certificates office listening to the city clerk say, "Look, I don't make up this stuff. It's right here on your birth certificate: 'Born to lose'." Does this mean that all these individuals can be helped? Probably not. But it is worth a try, since what is being done for them now does not work.

Individuals suffering from specific psychological reversal are not massively reversed but have reversals on one or several subjects. An individual can be very successful in everything in his or her life except one small thing. For instance, a student can excel in every subject but one. Dr. Callahan describes a 38 year old college student who was successful in all of her studies except chemistry. She just could not understand her chemistry. She had no trouble reading any other type of book. He treated her for her psychological reversal in this area, and she went on to be able to read and comprehend her chemistry books.

Other individuals may have several phobias or other problems. They may be reversed on each specific phobia or problem and should, therefore, be tested for psychological reversal before treatment begins. Any treatment will not work until the reversals have been treated first.

A mini-reversal can occur anywhere during the treatment process. As an individual begins to release his/her fear or anxiety, there is sometimes a tendency to want to hold on to at least some of the fear or anxiety. In other words, the individual does not let go completely. This is probably due to a fear of having to face the problem and not being able to imagine that it can be completely eliminated through treatment. Because of this, the individual becomes reversed, in some instances, numerous times before they finally release all the fear.

I remember treating a psychologist who constantly had "knots" in his stomach, which had been occurring for at least ten years. He attended a seminar that I was teaching in Minneapolis in 1988, and then asked to be treated privately. I asked him to quantify his anxiety regarding the knots on a scale of 1-10 with 10 being the most severe and 1 being completely relaxed. As we approached the lower numbers he suffered a mini-reversal, which was treated. He then progressed from a 3 to a 2.5, then to a 2. From that point, down to a 1, he suffered five or six mini-reversals before finally releasing all of the anxiety. Afterward he stated he had been treated by several colleagues over the years with little or no success. This was the first time he had ever felt absolutely no tension in his stomach.

There are many things that make a person susceptible to psychological reversal. Different people have different levels of susceptibility, and individuals have, within their lifetimes, varying degrees of susceptibility. The accumulation of stress is a major precursor. Individuals with a weak "psychological immune system" seem to be much more susceptible to reversals. Psychological reversal also seems to affect individuals more during negative times in their lives. But as they become more aware of themselves, learn more self acceptance, and change their life styles, the occurrence of psychological reversal diminishes (Callahan).

I have observed that psychological reversal occurs in all phases of life. It can be seen in the reluctance of the individual to seek help for physical, emotional or spiritual conditions. It can occur in education, raising children, employee-employer relationships, love relationships, sports activities when trying to excel, and in all kinds of interpersonal relationships. The bottom line is that all psychological reversals must be treated prior to administering treatment in other areas. Eliminating reversals facilitates and maximizes effective treatment and satisfying relationships.

Psychologically reversed individuals fear recovery because they know that if they recover from the phobia, anxiety or addiction, they will be able, or have to face whatever they were afraid of. As a result, a psychological reversal is sometimes created to prevent a cure.

For instance, one of my neighbors had planned to go on a Caribbean cruise. We live in Mesa, AZ, and the cruise started in Miami, FL. She was afraid of both flying and heights so she was going by bus. Can you imagine the long miles of a bus trip from Arizona to Florida? I suggested that she might be able to be cured of her fear of flying and heights. Her fear was so great that she couldn't imagine that it was possible, and she was afraid that even if she was treated, the fear might come back. Her comment was, "After I get back you can treat me!" Obviously, I didn't even have to test her for reversal; it was very apparent.

Callahan notes, "Many psychologists have stated over the years that certain patients want to be ill, or want to be disturbed, or want to die, even though they actively seek help. Freud postulated a "Death instinct" to account for this. Albert Ellis points out that most neurotics are self-sabotaging and self-defeating.

"Religions, too, are faced with believers who, despite their professed desire to live according to the precepts of their religion, still cannot seem to do it. The problem is among both laymen and leaders."

In Romans 7:18-20, this dilemma is presented in a religious context by Saint Paul.

(18) "For I know that in me (that is, in my flesh) dwelleth no good thing: for to will is present with me, but how to perform that which is good I find not.

(19) For the good that I would I do not; but the evil which I would not, that I do.

St. Paul proceeds to give an explanation for his dilemma that is still accepted today.

(20) Now if I do that I would not, it is no more I that do it, but sin that dwelleth in me.

(21) I find then a law, that, when I would do good, evil is present with me.

(22) For I delight in the law of God after the inward man:

(23) But I see another law in my members, warring against the law of my mind, and bringing me into captivity to the law of sin which is my members.

(24) Oh wretched man that I am! Who shall deliver me from the body of this death?"

From "The Living Bible" we find in Galatians 5:17:

"For we naturally love to do evil things that are just the opposite from the things that the Holy Spirit tells us to do; and the good things we want to do when the Spirit has His way with us are just the opposite of our natural desires. These two forces within us are constantly fighting each other to win control over us, and our wishes are never free from their pressures."

Callahan continues, "Thus, when a member of a religious group sins, he can explain his 'backsliding' by saying, 'The devil made me do it.' Yet, both this common (and sometimes humorous) phrase, and the classification of 'self-defeating' or 'self-destructive' given to some patients by frustrated therapists, are actually no more nor less than attempts to in some way make understandable what I now have identified as psychological reversal."

There are many grossly overweight people who are psychologically reversed and can not lose any weight, or who, if they do lose weight, gain it right back -- and then some. Others who are only about five to ten pounds overweight can not lose this small amount, but do not gain any more. Still others manage to lose most of the weight they want to but get within about ten pounds of their professed goals and stop. The latter group suffers from what Callahan calls a mini-reversal.

The most common type of reversal is one in which a person says, "I want to accomplish............" but does not achieve the desired goal. The next most common type is the person who consciously and subconsciously wants to accomplish the goal, but who will not take the necessary steps. The third type is one in which many different negative life beliefs have been inculcated into the individual, usually at an early age, by someone of authority. The beliefs that a person doesn't deserve happiness or success are examples of this type of upbringing. Others believe that they must be victims, must be used. They believe that they are incapable, dumb, inadequate, unworthy, worthless, have no identity, and the list goes on.

All attempts to treat a person who has any of these types of psychological reversals will end in failure if the psychological reversal is not treated first.

The diagnosis and treatment of these disorders will be explained fully in later chapters.

Chapter 6

Quality Muscle Testing

Manual muscle testing is a precise measure of a neurological response in the body. It is a test, not a contest between two individuals.

The idea is to determine if a muscle has the ability to "lock" or feel springy when manual pressure is applied. It takes practice but is easy to learn. The most common error is a tendency to overpower the individual being tested. Light to moderate pressure will give the best response.

As a tester, you must observe the size, age and strength of the person to be tested and use pressure suitable to the individual. Obviously, the same pressure would not be used on a frail person as would be used on an athlete.

The best muscle to test is the deltoid group of the shoulder, which holds the arm straight horizontal (parallel to the floor). Before testing, be sure to ask the person if he/she has any shoulder problem that might be aggravated by testing the arm. If so, use the opposite arm.

To test, stand facing the person and ask him/her to raise his/her left arm so it is parallel with the floor, if you are right handed. Have the person use his/her right arm if you are left handed. Be sure that the person's elbow is fully extended and the palm of his/her hand is facing down to the floor. (See Figure 6a)

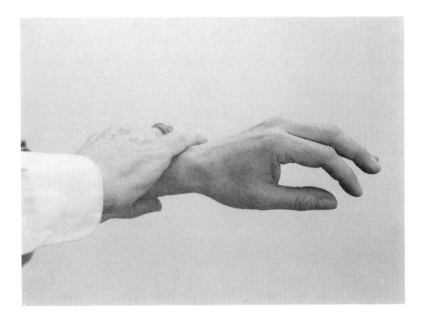

Figure 6a
Put your right hand on his/her left wrist and your left
hand on his/her right shoulder to stabilize. (See Figure 6b).

Figure 6b

Figure 6c

It is important to advise the person that you are going to begin the test and that he/she is to resist your pressure. Begin by applying five to fifteen pounds of pressure (depending on the strength of the person) gradually, so that the person can feel your pressure and begin resisting. Do not try to be too quick -- remember this is a test, not a contest. If the person's arm is weak, use his/her opposite arm.

If both arms are weak, and you are a chiropractic physician, find the reason and correct it. If you are layman or a doctor not familiar with the techniques of applied kinesiology you cannot correct the weak muscles. Refer the person to someone who can, or use a muscle that is strong such as the rectus femorus (thigh muscle) (See Figure 7a).

The rectus femorus is best tested in the sitting position. Ask the person to raise either the right or left knee about four inches. To stabilize the person, if you are right handed, place your left hand on his/her right shoulder and your right hand on the knee being tested. Apply gradual pressure, after you ask the person to resist to see if the knee "locks" or feels "springy" and can't be pushed down. If not, try the other knee.

Figure 7a

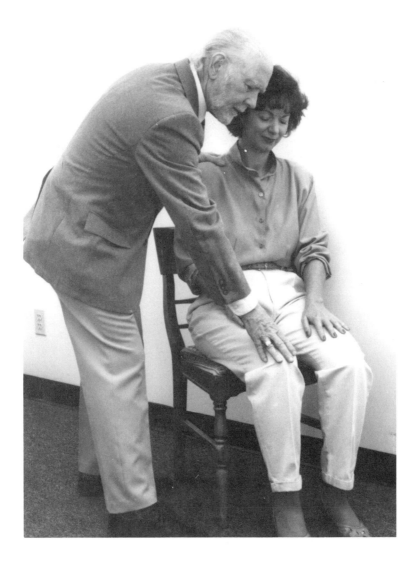

Figure 7b

Now that you have a strong muscle to use as an indicator, have the person think of their fear, anxiety, compulsion, experience or addictive urge and test the muscle again. It should become weaker. In some cases, it will feel like all the strength just disappeared. (See Figure 6c or 7b).

In others there will be a spongy feeling, or a feeling somewhere in between the two. After practicing, you will become proficient at telling the difference. The most frequent error is applying too much force. Once again, this is a test, not a contest! On the other hand, some testers do not apply enough pressure and cannot detect any weakness. Unless a person has neurological disorganization (described in Chapter 9), there should be a detectable weakening in the muscle when the person thinks of his/her fear, anxiety, compulsion or addictive urge, etc.

To illustrate to the person that anxiety will weaken a muscle, ask the person to state his/her name. Test the indicator muscle and it will remain strong. Next, ask the person to state his/her name, but instruct him/her to give you a fictitious name the second time. Immediately test the same indicator muscle. It should feel weak or at least spongy. Ask the person if he/she felt the difference (this should be obvious). If the person does notice the difference, explain that is how the body reacts to anxiety.

If the person indicates that he/she did not feel any difference, but you noticed that there definitely was, repeat the procedure until the person gets in tune with his/her body and really does feel the difference.

Chapter 7

Therapy Localization

The various types of energy flowing through the body have not been completely explained by science. Many researchers have measured these energies. In his studies of the healing power of the body, Becker describes the effects of the loss of energy in the non-union of bone fractures. Nordenstrom, a Norwegian radiologist, has been studying the existence of energies in the human body for twenty years. Rawls and Davis have studied electromagnetic balance and imbalance. Acupuncture meridian resistance and its relationship to physiologic changes in the body has been measured by the Ryodoraku method.

In her search for answers to how certain individuals can see auras and vortices of force surrounding the body, Shafica Karagulla, M.D. has studied this phenomena intensively. The general public has seen the energy on television, captured in picture form, by Kirlian photography.

The healing professions use EKG's to measure the electro potential of the heart as a guide to diagnosing. Electroencephlographs are used for brain wave studies.

D.D. Palmer, the discoverer of modern day Chiropractic, spoke frequently of energies and the importance of their balance in the body. He said in his book The Chiropractic Adjuster, "Too much or not enough energy is disease."

With all the sophisticated instruments that have been developed and are being developed, the human body is still extraordinarily precise. In 1974 Goodheart examined a patient with a carpal tunnel syndrome. Wanting to demonstrate that there was a mechanical distortion of the bones of the wrist, he asked the patient to put her hand around the wrist and squeeze the bones together. He then tested the strength of the hand using the thumb and little finger held together tightly by the patient. Noticing the strengthening of the hand muscles he told his patient, "See, if you hold the bones of your wrist together, your hand becomes strong!" The patient replied, "But Dr. Goodheart, I wasn't squeezing the wrist, I was only holding it lightly." He immediately wondered, why was that? He then asked the patient to lightly touch the wrist with her finger tips; he got the same results. From that observation, he then tried the same approach with different parts of the body, and found that if there was a weak muscle and the appropriate treatment point was touched by the patient, the muscle would strengthen as long as the point was touched. Conversely, he found that if a strong muscle was used as an indicator, if any point on the body was touched that needed treatment, or that had something wrong, the previously strong muscle would weaken. He termed this new observation "Therapy Localization."

To use therapy localization to locate a person's diagnostic and treatment points, the examiner will generally start with a strong indicator muscle, usually the arm (See Figure 6b). The person will then be asked to think of his/her anxiety, phobia or addictive substance, etc; when tested, the muscle will weaken (See Figure 6c). The person is then asked to place his/her hand on a specific test point (See Figure 7c which illustrates touching test point 1, as shown in Figure 8a). If it is the correct point, the muscle will immediately strengthen. The same will be true if the person places his/her hand on the actual corresponding treatment point. (See treatment point 1 just below the eyes in Figure 8b) We will go into greater detail on each individual problem as you progress through the book.

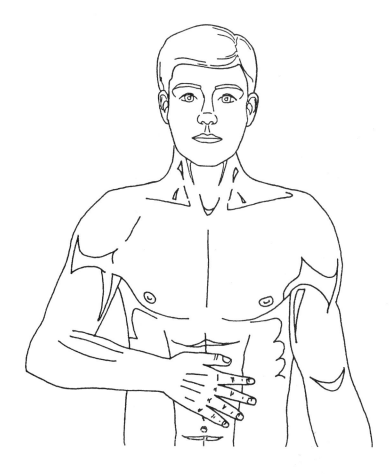

Figure 7c

Chapter 8

Meridian Therapy, aka Acupuncture, Acupressure

Some 5,000 years ago the Chinese began observing a phenomenon of energy in the body that they eventually called CHI (pronounced chee), which means "life force." They found this energy flowed through the body from the chest to the hands, from the hands to the head, from the head to the feet and then back to the chest. They found that there were no anatomical channels (tube-like conduits) as there are with arteries. However, the energy seemed to flow along particular lines or pathways called meridians.

They found there were points along these energy meridians that, when stimulated, could balance or transfer energies to make them flow freely and evenly, restoring normal function to various parts of the body. This could be accomplished by several methods, including using finger pressure, using sharp bamboo slivers, using fish bones, burning of herbal substances (moxibustion) on the skin surface, and using metal needles. Over the years, the various points along each meridian were numbered and named in accordance with what occurred and what organs were affected when they were stimulated.

It was also observed that each of the meridians had a specific emotion connected with it, and that if a person had an over or under abundance of that emotion, balancing the energies could restore the person's normal emotional balance.

The work of a North Korean, Professor Kim Bong Han, was reported by William Tiller of Stanford University in his book, The Kirlian Aura. Kim injected radioactive phosphors into an acupuncture point and followed it by using special instruments to record its path. He found that it proceeded along the path which was described by the Chinese, although there were no known anatomical channels such as arteries, veins or lymphatic ducts.

The Norwegian scientist, Dr. Bjorn Nordenstrom has also studied electromagnetic energies, and found that the meridians of the body are apparently electromagnetic.

Robert O. Becker, M.D., an orthopedist, in his book The Body Electric describes the electromagnetic nature of the body and how this affects us specifically and generally.

Richard Gerber, M.D., in his book Vibrational Medicine devotes an entire chapter to acupuncture, which he titles, "Subtle-Energy Systems & Their Relevance to Ancient Approaches Toward Healing."

In 1966 Goodheart began to study acupuncture and found that various muscles were associated with specific energy organ meridians. He began to use acupuncture long before President Nixon's trip to China, which first prompted western medicine's interest in acupuncture.

At a 1974, I.C.A.K. meeting in Florida, Pearlman presented a paper describing the electromagnetic nature of the acupuncture energy, and the "antenna" effect of the acupuncture needle. He demonstrated the paper's finding by manually muscle testing a subject. He found a specific muscle to be weak, then inserted a steel acupuncture needle in the tonify point of the corresponding meridian; the muscle became strong. Next he put a leaded ceramic cup over the needle; and the muscle immediately became weak again. He then tested a strong muscle and inserted a needle in the sedate point of the corresponding meridian; the muscle became weak. When he placed the leaded ceramic cup over the needle the muscle became strong again.

This showed the antenna effect of needles and other stimulation that draws electromagnetic energy into the body and affects the meridian.

Goodheart found that another way of stimulating the various points of the energy meridians was to percuss (tap) the point with the finger tip. He described the procedure as a way to relieve pain and presented his results in 1979 at the annual summer meeting of the I.C.A.K.

As was previously mentioned, the Chinese found that specific meridians were associated with specific emotions. The following listing shows the meridians and their most common corresponding emotions:

Energy Meridian - Emotion

Kidney - Fear
Bladder - Miffed
Heart - Overjoyed
Small Intestine - Lost or Vulnerable
Triple Warmer (Triple Heater, Thyroid) - Muddled thinking
Circulation - Sex (Pericardium), Instability, Non-thinking,
Non-emotive
Gall Bladder - Resentment
Liver - Anger
Lung - Grief
Large Intestine - Dogmatically positioned
Stomach - Disgust
Spleen - Low Self Esteem

This does not mean the emotion that the doctor thinks a person is suffering from is the correct one, or that the corresponding organ should always be treated. You learned in Chapter 7 that the most accurate way to diagnose what the person needs is by therapy localization. **You must always treat what the person's body says it wants, not what you think it needs.** Setting our personal egos aside may be difficult for those who were trained in the traditional methods of diagnosis.

But for those who learn to accept that "the body knows," there will be a realization of existing powers that are far greater than our educated minds. In accepting this, we will be grateful for the results of the treatment.

Now that we have explored the scientific basis for acupuncture energies, we are ready to learn how to apply this knowledge in a practical way. To do this, we will use the muscle testing procedures explained in Chapter 6. The process that follows will be explained in step-by-step detail in Chapter 10.

When a person thinks of a specific event, issue, phobia, desire, or behavior and his/her arm muscle weakens when tested manually, he/she is instructed to place the opposite hand on each one of the meridian test (alarm) points in sequence, to find the one that will negate the weakness.(See Figure 8a for location of these test points).

As soon as the test point is located, find the corresponding treatment points (See Figure 8b for location of the treatment points).

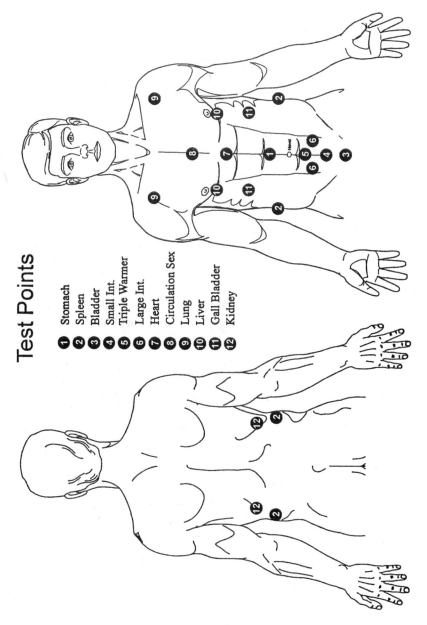

Figure 8a

Treatment Points

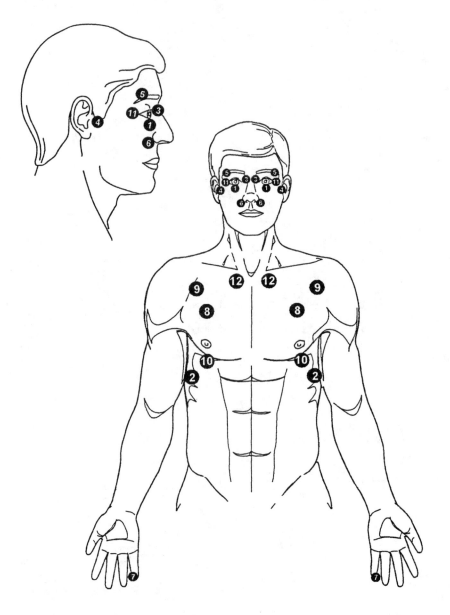

Figure 8b

The person is then requested to quantify the intensity of the emotion on a scale of 1 to 10, 10 being the highest and 1 being total relaxation. The rating as shown in Figure 9 is adapted from Callahan.

10.	My discomfort is the worst it can possibly be. It is intolerable. It puts me in a panic.
9.	My Discomfort is very close to intolerable.
8.	My discomfort is very severe.
7.	My discomfort is severe.
6.	My discomfort is very uncomfortable.
5.	My discomfort is uncomfortable, but I can stand it.
4.	My discomfort is noticeable and bothersome, but I can stand it.
3.	I feel a slight degree of discomfort, but I am totally in control.
2.	I'm rather calm, quite relaxed, with no discomfort.
1.	I'm totally relaxed, perfectly calm.

Figure 9

Note: the word "discomfort" is interchangeable with fear, obsession, addiction, urge, desire or whatever negative or upsetting emotion is being felt at the time.

The person is then tested to determine if there is any psychological reversal, which should be treated immediately. Detailed instructions on the diagnosis and treatment of psychological reversal will follow in Chapter 9. The person is now ready to begin the basic treatment as described in Chapter 10.

The treatment as described in Chapter 10 is done by the person being treated. He/she will be tapping specific acupuncture treatment points.

The tapping is a stimulation of an acupuncture point to balance the subtle energies of the body so the person can go from an anxiety mode to a problem solving mode that will allow him/her to become completely relaxed.

The person is instructed to keep thinking of their fear, anxiety, compulsion, or urges and reminded constantly to continually keep their mind on the problem. As the tapping proceeds and the person becomes freed from his/her problem, it is harder for him/her to keep his/her mind on the problem.

Chapter 9

Neurological Disorganization, Psychological Reversal

A certain percentage of individuals do not appear to respond to normal muscle testing. For instance, as was pointed out in Chapter 5, when an individual makes a statement that is false or that causes anxiety, there should be a weakening of the previously strong arm (See Figures 6b&c). A person will be strong to a true statement such as "My name is John", if that is actually his name. Conversely, he should become weak if he says, "My name is George," and his name is not George. However, if a person has what we call neurological disorganization, he will be strong on both statements.

When a person is first introduced to this method of treatment, it is best to explain that a new and different method of diagnosis and treatment is going to be used, which involves his/her nervous system. Explain that the muscle system acts very much like a polygraph, which records differences in blood pressure, heart rate, breathing and respiration rate. The difference is that in this case, a muscle controlled by the nervous system will weaken if anything is said or thought that causes anxiety. Ask for, and receive, permission to demonstrate the procedure.

Demonstrate by saying to the person, "I know your name but please say to me, "My name is_____." Then, immediately test a previously tested strong muscle. It will be strong. Now ask the person, "Is that strong?" Wait for an answer. Now have the person say, "My name is _____" (give a fictitious name for them to say) and retest the previously strong muscle. It should now weaken. Ask the person, "Is your arm strong or weak?" Wait for an answer. This is to determine if the person really understands what is happening. You will be surprised that some individuals, after their arm weakens, answer that they don't know whether or not their arm is weak! If this happens, you must repeat the sequence so that the person understands that if their arm weakens after making a false statement or thinks of something that causes anxiety, that the nervous system does react by a weakening of a previously strong muscle.

If the muscle stays strong on both statements, the person is neurologically disorganized. This must be treated first, or you will not have a valid test instrument (the individual's nervous system).

The preceding test can be done with any set of statements, one being true and the other being false.

Neurological disorganization is diagnosed with a sequence of forty simple tests originally conceived and developed by Callahan. These can be performed in less than two minutes, as follows.

1. Have the person touch (therapy localize) the K-27 (See Figure 10) on the right (See Figure 10a) with right hand, palm down and test a strong muscle against the following phases of respiration:

(1) Normal Respiration.
(2) Full breath in.
(3) One half breath out.
(4) Full breath out.
(5) One half breath in.

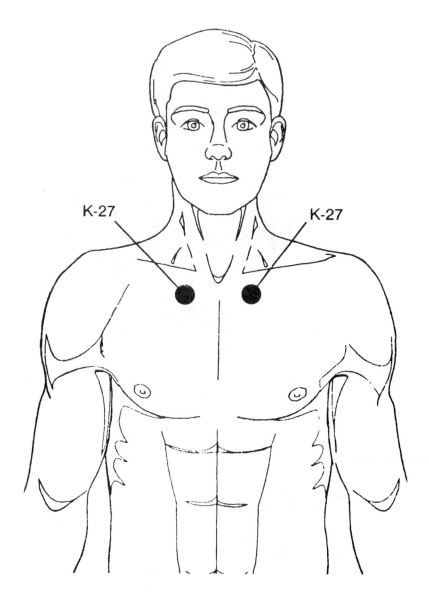

Figure 10

Figure 10a

Figure 10b

Figure 10c

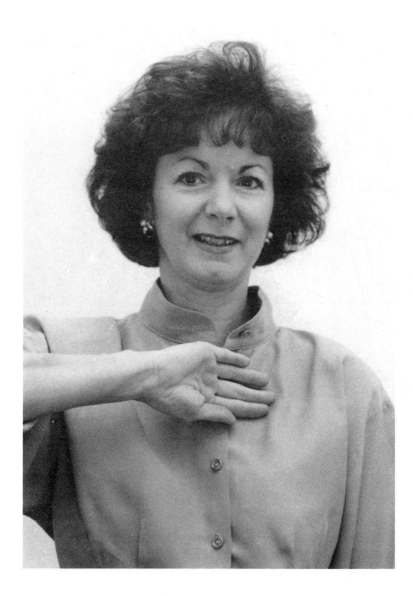

Figure 10d

Figure 10e

Figure 10f

Figure 10g

Figure 10h

If the muscle weakens on any phase of respiration, treat it as follows: Have the person continue to therapy localize K-27 and hold the phase of respiration while you tap the Brain Balance point, (See Figure 11) on the opposite hand just behind the knuckles between the 4th and 5th metacarpal bones for five seconds.

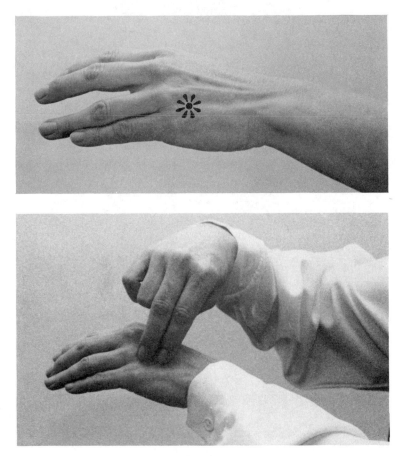

Figure 11

Retest in the same phase of respiration to check if correction was made - that is, see if the muscle is now strong on that phase of respiration while therapy localizing K-27. If not, continue tapping until it is done. Continue to test and treat, if necessary, until all five phases of respiration have been completed.

2. Have the person continue to therapy localize the right K- 27, but this time palm up (back of the hand touching), (See Figure 10b) and repeat the five phases of respiration. Treat as required.

3. Have person therapy localize the K-27 on the left, with the right hand, palm down, (See Figure 10c) and repeat testing all five phases of respiration. Treat as required.

4. Have the person continue to therapy localize the left K-27 with the right hand, but this time palm up (back of hand touching) (See Figure 10d) and test all five phases of respiration. Treat as required.

Now, repeat the entire sequence using the left hand on the left K-27 palm down, (See Figure 10e) then palm up, (See Figure 10f) then the left hand on the right K-27, palm down (See Figure 10g) and then palm up (See Figure 10h) using the five phases of respiration as previously described. Treat as required.

As I mentioned previously, this seemingly long procedure takes less that two minutes once you become familiar with the steps. After you have corrected the neurological disorganization, retest the person having him/her state the false statement. This time a strong muscle should weaken.

MASSIVE PSYCHOLOGICAL REVERSAL

Massive Psychological reversal, as mentioned in Chapter 5, must be treated before treatment of any kind can be effective.

Massive Psychological Reversal is when the individual is negative about almost everything, about life and happiness. It is when the person says, "I want to be happy" and their strong indicator muscle weakens, but will remain strong when saying, " I want to be miserable."

It is possible to test for this without having the person say the words. Have him/her place the palm of their hand on the top of the head and the strong indicator muscle will stay strong. Then have him/her turn the hand over and place the back of the hand on top of their head and the strong indicator muscle will become weak. To put it in a way that is easily re-membered, "palm is power, back is slack." This test shows that the person is NOT massively psychologically reversed. If the indicator muscle weakens when the hand is placed palm down on the head and stays strong while placing the back of the hand on the head, this person IS massively psychologically reversed.

Now it is time to demonstrate to him/her that they have massive psychological reversal, by showing them that saying "I want to be happy" will cause them to weaken, and that saying, "I want to be miserable" will make them stay strong.

If the individual is strong on both palm down and palm up he/she has neurological disorganization and the procedures described in the beginning of this chapter must be done before any further testing or treatment is attempted.

To treat massive psychological reversal, instruct the person to tap on the psychological reversal point on the side of either hand (See Figures 12 a&b), (whichever is most comfort-able depending on whether the person is right or left handed) between the beginning of the little finger and the wrist while saying, "I deeply accept myself even though I am miserable." Repeat this at least three times and instruct the individual to do this at least once every waking hour every day for a week.

It is usually necessary to have them take Rescue Rem-edy or MinTran or MinBall which is discussed on the last page of this chapter.

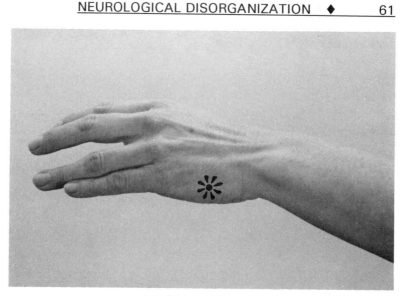

Figure 12a

Figure 12b

PSYCHOLOGICAL REVERSAL

The difference between massive psychological reversal and ordinary psychological reversal is a matter of degree. Ordinary psychological reversal is usually limited to one or a small number of issues.

If a strong muscle tests weak when a person makes a statement that he/she wants to accomplish a particular goal, this illustrates that he/she has a psychological reversal. This shows that the statement made by the person causes anxiety.

For instance, I had a patient who was overweight and had been dieting on his own for a long time with no permanent results. I asked him to make the statement, "I want to lose weight," and I tested a strong muscle. Much to his surprise his arm weakened. He then said, "But I really do want to lose weight." I tested him again and his arm still weakened. I explained to him that for whatever reason, his subconscious mind did not believe the statement, and therefore his muscle weakened. Next, I asked him to make the statement, "I want to gain weight." He was retested immediately and to his surprise, his arm stayed strong! I explained that this statement was in agreement with his subconscious, and that was the reason he could never keep weight off for very long.

To treat the psychological reversal, I instructed him to tap the psychological reversal point on the side of his hand between the wrist and the beginning of the little finger, the karate chop part of the hand, (See Figure 12a&b), while saying, "I deeply accept myself, even though I am overweight." I had him repeat this three times while tapping.

I asked him to again make the statement, "I want to lose weight." This time he remained strong.

There is another degree of psychological reversal. This is when a person tests strong when he/she says he/she wants to accomplish a goal, but when the statement is changed to I *will* lose weight rather than I *want* to lose weight, the person's muscle will test weak. These are two separate issues. If this happens, the affirmation while tapping the psychological reversal point should be changed to, "I deeply accept myself even if I never lose weight or never stop smoking or never accomplish _____."

The mind is very literal and statements made by the individual being tested must be very precise. Here is a list of statements that can be applied to all degrees of psychological reversals.

I want to _____

I will_____

I will do the things necessary to_____

I will allow myself to_____

I deserve to_____

It is possible for me to_____

Doing (overcoming) this will be good for me.

Doing (overcoming) this will be good for others.

It will be safe for me to do this.

If the person weakens on any of these statements, he/she is psychologically reversed and an appropriate self acceptance affirmation must be made up to say while tapping on the psychological reversal point.

In some individuals the treatment for psychological reversal lasts only about thirty seconds, so the treatment for the phobia, anxiety or addiction or whatever, must be done very quickly to be effective. In some individuals, there is a tendency to frequently revert back into psychological reversal. (The person does not make any progress by tapping the regular treatment points.) If this happens there is another step to the treatment. Find the interspace between the 2nd and 3rd rib next to the sternum (See Figure 13); it will therapy localize and also be very tender. This is the treatment point for recurring psychological reversals.

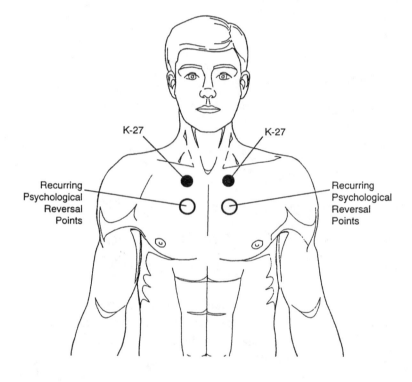

Figure 13

Stimulate this point with a firm rotary massage for about 20 to 30 seconds, while stating the affirmation.

In addition it will be very helpful to have the person take Bach Rescue Remedy, usually about five drops every waking hour, or MinTran or MinBall, two tablet three times a day, as he/she taps on the psychological reversal point repeating the affirmation, with feeling, three times.

Rescue Remedy is a combination of five Bach Flower Remedies, of which there are thirty eight. These were discovered and developed by an English physician, Edward Bach, in 1928. They are available from most health food stores or can be ordered from Ellon Bach USA, Inc, 644 Merrick Rd., Lynbrook, NY 11563. Additional uses of these and other flower remedies will be discussed in later chapters. Flower remedies are not drugs, nor do they cause drug-like actions or side effects. They work subtly to help the body return to a balanced energy state, complementing the acupuncture system.

If the administration of Bach Rescue Remedy does not seem to have long lasting results, six tablets a day of a nutritional product called MinTran produced by Standard Process Company, Palmyra, WI 53156 has been found to be very effective. I owe this information to Lorraine Dumas, D.C., of Nokomis, FL.

Dr. Dumas received the information from the research of D.A. Versendaal, D.C., the developer of Contact Reflex Analysis. Versendaal found that MinTran supported brain function. Another similar product is MinBall, supplied by Nutri-West, P.O. Box 1298, Douglas, WY 82633.

It appears that there is no permanent "cure" to psychological reversal, because the accumulation of stress seems to exacerbate it under certain conditions. Everybody should be tested for it before any treatment.

In addition, there is another type of psychological reversal discovered and named by Callahan as a "mini psychological reversal." This is a condition which occurs during the treatment process when the person stops progressing.

When a person has a mini reversal, he/she will progress from a high degree of fear or anxiety to a lower degree, but then cease all progress. For instance, on a scale of one to ten, with ten being the highest, a person stops progress at six and can't get any lower. This is an example of a mini reversal. To diagnose it, have the person say, "I want to get lower than a six in my fear (anxiety, desire, etc.) of/for___." Test the indicator muscle; if it weakens, there is a mini reversal. To treat, simply have the individual repeat three times, "I deeply accept myself even though I can't get below a six on this fear (anxiety, desire, etc)." while tapping on the psychological reversal point (See Figures 12 a&b). Retest the person; the indicator muscle should be strong. This diagnosis and treatment will be restated in the treatment chapters several times for your convenience.

Chapter 10

The Basic Acu-POWER Treatment

After testing for neurological disorganization and psychological reversal, and treating each as necessary, it is now possible to start the actual treatment. Remember, without taking care of neurological disorganization, your testing will not be accurate. And, without treating the psychological reversal, your treatment will not be successful.

To begin, have the person think about his/her fear, anxiety or urge. Quantify the degree which he/she suffers from the problem by using the scale of one to ten - ten being the worst (highest) and one being totally relaxed, as described in Figure 9.

As soon as the person states, "I am at '9'." for example, test the strong arm (See Figure 6b) to determine if the statement is correct. Usually it will test strong indicating a correct statement; however, if the strong arm becomes weak (See Figure 6c), the number selected is not correct. You must then ask the person to say, "I am at '10'" or "I am at '8'," and then retest. A number on either side of the original guess will probably be the correct one, as most individuals are not more than one number off. On rare occasions, when the individual has very little self awareness, you will have to go on a hunting expedition to find the correct degree of fear. Occasionally, a person will be so out of touch with himself/herself, or so distraught (feeling he/she is incapable of thinking clearly enough to quantify the correct degree of fear or discomfort) that you will have to begin by asking the person to say, "I'm at '10'," and then test. If that is not true, that is, if his/her arm weakens, have the person continue to go down the scale from '10' until he/she reaches a number at which their arm stays strong. This is the person's degree of fear or discomfort; now you have a measuring point with which to gage the person's progress or lack of it.

Next, have the individual think about the fear, anxiety or urge. Test the person's strong arm, and it should weaken. Ask him/her to continue to think of their fear or anxiety and have him/her touch test point one, located just above the navel (See Figure 8a), with their free hand, then test the previously weakened arm. If it becomes strong, you have found the correct energy meridian. You can now locate the treatment point on Figure 8b. (Note that in this illustration, the treatment point is on a different part of the body than the test point for the energy meridian. In some instances, however, the treatment points and test point are the same.).

If touching test point '1' while he/she was thinking of the fear, anxiety or urge did not make the arm strong, then progress to test point '2' and continue through the test points until you find the meridian test point that makes the test arm becomes strong. Find the corresponding treatment points on Figure 8b, and instruct the person to tap the treatment points with the index or middle finger of each hand for ten to fifteen seconds while thinking of their fear, anxiety or urge. After the allotted time, instruct the person to stop and quantify the degree of fear, anxiety or urge. It usually will have gone down at least two points, if it started above a '6'.

Occasionally, if the person originally quantified the degree of fear, anxiety or urge at a '6' or '7' for example, but quantified it higher after thinking of it some more while tapping, it means that they were not really concentrating on the subject with enough intensity to correctly quantify it. This is usually because thinking about the problem is painful, and he/she wants to avoid that pain. (They have been there before and it hurts!) The first time this occurred while I was treating a patient, I wasn't quite sure of what to do. I persisted in the treatment, and after a rise from '7' to a '10', my patient's continued tapping gradually lowered the number to the original starting point and finally to a one.

There is a strong probability that this will happen to you, too. Explain to the person that there is nothing wrong with the testing procedure, and that he/she just wasn't concentrating hard enough on the subject at first because of the pain he/she knew would occur.

If a person comes down from '10' to '7' for instance, and stops progress after two additional tapping segments, it means that he/she has suffered a mini reversal on the subject. These occur when individuals are so afraid of the subject that they cannot even imagine not being afraid, and do not want to be exposed to the subject, even on a trial basis. It is a form, albeit irrational, of the fear of fear.

Test the person by having him/her say, "I want to get below '7' on my fear of(urge for, etc.)____." If the arm weakens, it confirms that he/she does indeed have a mini-psychological reversal.

Treat this by having the person tap on the psychological reversal point on the side of the hand (See Figures 12a&b), while repeating three times, "I deeply accept myself even though I can't get below a '7' on my fear of (urge for)____." Retest by having the person say, "I want to get below '7' on this fear"(urge). If he/she still tests weak, repeat the mini-psychological reversal treatment until the arm stays strong on testing for the reversal. Occasionally, if the reversals continue, there will be a need for rescue remedy or treatment of the recurring reversal points, which will be described later.

Have the person continue to tap on the original treatment points. The degree of fear, anxiety or urge should decrease progressively to '1'. If it does not, and there is no mini psychological reversal, and he/she still tests strong while touching either the original test or treatment point while thinking of their fear, anxiety or urge, it is time to balance the right and left side of the brain. This treatment procedure was also conceived and developed by Callahan which he named the "gamut" treatment. In deference to him I call it the Brain Balance Treatment. Its purpose is to balance the front and back brain and the left and right brain to create an unimpeded communication through the corpus callosum (the nerve fibers that connect the brain hemispheres).

The treatment consists of nine steps which can be completed in just thirty seconds. The steps are illustrated beginning on the next page.

While the person is thinking of his/her fear, anxiety or urge, he/she proceeds as follows:

With each step, the person taps on the interspace one-half inch behind the forth and fifth knuckles of the left or right hand (this is the Brain Balance Point) for approximately three seconds. In acupuncture this point is known as Triple Warmer 3 (See Figure 11).

BRAIN BALANCE TREATMENT

Step 1. With eyes open.

Step 2. With eyes closed.

Step 3. With eyes open, point eyes down and to the left without moving the head.

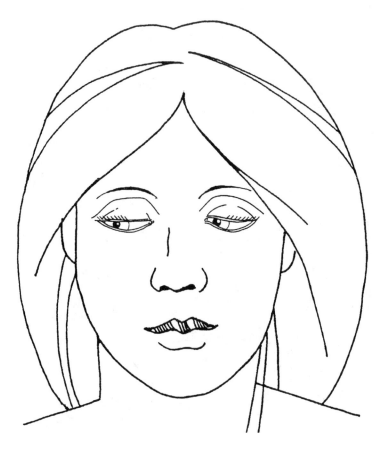

Step 4. With eyes open, point eyes down and to the right without moving the head.

Step 5. With eyes open, roll eyes in large circles in a clockwise rotation.

Step 6. With eyes open, roll eyes in large circles in a counter-
clockwise rotation.

Step 7. With eyes open, hum any tune such as Happy Birthday, Yankee Doodle, or make up a tune.

Step 8. With eyes open, count to ten.

Step 9. With eyes open, hum again as in step 7.

This procedure allows the imagination (right) side of the brain to communicate with the logical (left) side of the brain and allows the memory (front) portion of the brain to communicate with the present time (back) portion of the brain, bringing all portions of the brain into balance so logic and imagination can be in tune with present and past memory.

An interesting anecdotal incident occurred when I was treating a woman for her fear of flying. She did not come down from her '10' after about a minute of tapping on the regular treatment point. She was not psychologically reversed. She was then instructed to go through the Brain Balance procedure, and as she was doing this, I was explaining to her husband that this part of the treatment was to improve or restore communication between her right and left brain. Hearing this she stopped the treatment and said, "You know, for years, since I was in grade school, I always knew that I was thinking with just one side of my brain at a time - I could actually feel or sense it. When I was doing any mathematical figuring or logical thinking, I could actually feel the thought process going on in the left side of my brain, and if I was imagining or doing art work or musical expression, I could feel it going on in the right side of my brain!" After the treatment was completed and she had eliminated her fear of flying, she said, " For the first time in my memory, I no longer feel that I am using only one side of my brain when I am thinking. It sure feels good!"

This was the first time I had ever observed this but I would imagine there are others who have had similar experiences.

On completion of the Brain Balance treatment, the individuals will usually experience '1' to '2' point drops in their fears, anxieties or addictive urges. If the fear, anxiety or addictive urge has not completely dropped to a '1', instruct the person to continue thinking of the fear, anxiety or urge and tap on the original treatment points.

If continued tapping does not bring the fear, anxiety or urge down to a '1', and he/she is not reversed and you have had them preform the Brain Balance treatment with no additional progress, the person has switched to a different facet of the fear, anxiety or urge. Instruct the person to think of the fear, anxiety or urge and have him/her touch the original test point. You will note that this will no longer make the arm strong. Instruct the person to touch test point '2' (See Figure 8a) and retest the indicator arm. If this makes it strong, find the treatment points approximately five inches below the arm pit on both sides of the chest (See Figure 8b) and instruct the person to think of the fear, anxiety or urge and tap the new treatment points.

If touching test point '2' did not strengthen the indicator arm, have the person progressively touch each test point in sequence (while thinking of their fear, anxiety or urge) while you test the indicator arm. As soon as the indicator arm strengthens, find the new set of corresponding treatment points (See Figures 8a and 8b).

Instruct the person to continue tapping the new treatment points until he/she gets down to a '1'.

The person may suffer another mini-reversal, and on rare occasions may switch to still another facet of the fear, anxiety or urge, in which case you would repeat the testing procedure as described previously.

Recurring psychological reversals may occur despite the continued tapping of the psychological reversal point and giving Rescue Remedy (five drops under the tongue). In this case, have the person therapy localize (touch) the recurring reversal points on either side of the sternum between the second and third rib as shown in Figure 13. There will be a weakening of the indicator arm on one or both recurring psychological reversal points. Have the person stimulate the side, or sides that therapy localized, by rubbing the area vigorously for twenty seconds while saying, "I deeply accept myself even though_____". It is also useful to recommend Rescue Remedy at this time (five drops under the tongue).

The use of MinTran from Standard Process or MinBall from Nutri-West (one or two tablets three times a day) may also be necessary in treating difficult cases.

Immediately after treating the recurring psychological reversal point(s), continue with tapping the previous treatment point. In some cases, as the person gets closer and closer to completely releasing the fear, anxiety or urge, he/she may make only very small increments of progress. For instance, the person may say, "I'm '1' or '2'." Test for a one and you will probably find that he/she is not there yet, as evidenced by a weak arm. The person will probably do the same when stating that he/she is a '2'. In this case have him/her say, "I'm at a '1 and 1/2'." Test, and this is probably where he/she is. This situation was described in Chapter 5, in which a psychologist who had been suffering from a long standing tightness in his gut became mini reversed five times when going from a '2' to a '1'. We went through '2', '1 and 3/4', '1 and 1/2', '1 and 1/4', and '1 and 1/8' before he was finally able to release all the tension!

The basic Acu-POWER treatment can be used for all types of phobias, anxieties, addictions, compulsive behaviors and post traumatic stress disorders. Its skillful use can, in many cases, be the only type of treatment needed. However, in some cases traditional counseling may be necessary as well. Many psychologists and counselors use the treatment in combination with traditional therapy and find that it reduces treatment time and improves the end results. They also find that the muscle testing gives them a "direct line" to their patient's real problem. Your body knows!

Chapter 11

Negative Life Beliefs

"Under all that we think, lives all we believe, like the ultimate veil of our spirits."

Antonio Machado

"We are what we think. All that we are
arises With our thoughts. With our
thoughts, We make our world."

The Buddha

In addition to psychological reversals - massive, first
and second degree, and mini, there are other stumbling blocks
that prevent people from achieving the maximum benefits of
their treatment, and their maximum enjoyment of life. These
stumbling blocks are negative life beliefs.

Negative life beliefs generally come from some real or
imagined remark, pronouncement or anything else said to, or
overheard by, the person -- usually coming from someone in
authority.

This authority is usually a parent but can be a relative,
teacher, clergyman/woman, police officer, employer, employee

or anyone else whom the person regards as authoritative or knowledgeable.

We have all heard the remarks, such as, "You'll never amount to anything," "you're worthless," "you're a nobody," "you're bad," "life is to be hard," "you're the cause of_____," "you don't deserve_____," "you're a born loser," etc. The pathetic part of this is that society makes fun of those individuals. I refer again to the syndicated single panel cartoon on the comics page called "Charlie", drawn by Rodrigeus, in which Charlie is standing in front of the counter of the birth certificate office listening the city clerk say, "Look - I don't make up this stuff. It's right there on your birth certificate: 'Born to lose'."

Depending on the time and circumstances and by whom the negative remark was made, the person to whom the remark was addressed may consider the insult to be true. From then on, the negative remark becomes imbedded in that person's system of beliefs and inculcated into his/her personality. Beliefs have the power to create (positive) and the power to destroy (negative).

We have all seen the comic strip "The Born Loser." From time to time most of us feel like we, too, are born losers. (Although we are more apt to "see" someone we know.) That is why the strip has the popularity and lasted as long as it has.

Anthony Robbins says in his book <u>Awaken the Giant Within</u>, "We all will act consistently with our views of who we truly are, whether that view is accurate or not. The reason is that one of the strongest forces in the human organism is the need for consistency." If we view ourselves with negative labels we will act out negative roles.

Among many of my patients who have had negative life beliefs, one woman stands out in my mind. She originally visited my office because of constant fatigue. Noting that she was 42 years old, divorced and had six children, I asked how she   was managing. She replied that it was a struggle because the father of the children was not paying the court ordered child support payments. When I asked if she was doing anything about it, that is, reporting this to the Clerk of Court, she said that she hadn't for a while, as it was useless anyway.

Asking her further questions, I discovered she had been married seven times. Her first marriage, at age 21, ended in less than a year. She then married a man whom we'll call 'Joe', who was the father of all her children, and divorced him. Then she married her third husband, a man whom we'll call 'Bill'. She divorced again, remarried 'Joe', her second (the father of the children), a marriage which again ended in divorce. She remarried 'Bill', divorced and then remarried him again, divorced him again and finally married husband four, whom we'll call 'Harry', a marriage which lasted only a few months.

This is when she came to see me. After hearing a number of the things which she had allowed to happen to her, it was apparent to me that this patient had a number of negative life beliefs. We discovered that she regarded herself as: unworthy, powerless, a victim, undeserving, used and deserving of punishment! No wonder her life turned out as it had. She repeatedly chose men who would make her negative beliefs come true!

She was, and is, physically attractive and in good physical shape. She also has, from what I could ascertain in the office, a pleasant demeanor. She appeared to be a concerned and caring mother of her children, one of whom has a brain injury from a near drowning accident. She practices her religion conscientiously but is not a "fanatic."

In order to discover her life beliefs, I tested her on each of the following belief systems which were originally compiled by Dr. Terry Franks. This was accomplished by having her verbalize each of the following statements and then testing a strong muscle.

NEGATIVE LIFE BELIEFS

I am:

unworthy
unlovable
powerless
guilty
worthless
alone
a victim
vulnerable
incompetent
misunderstood
abandoned
betrayed
inferior
sinful
separated from God
unproductive
unattractive
trapped
incapable
bad
undeserving
confused
a burden
dumb
used
unteachable
a failure

I have:

no soul
no identity

I deserve:

pain
punishment
failure

I cause:

misfortune
separation

In her case, she tested strong on the negative beliefs mentioned previously. To test someone, have him/her say each statement. Whichever statement results in the arm staying strong is a statement which the person believes to be true on a subconscious level, and possibly on a conscious level as well.

Before performing this test, it is necessary to explain to the person what you are trying to discover and why. Be sure to ask for permission.

Once you have established which, if any, negative belief(s) the person has, you can determine which energy meridian is out of balance. To do this, have the person state the opposite of the negative life belief. This will make the arm weak, and then you should have the person therapy localize each test point, until one point abolishes the weakness. For instance, if the person was strong on the statement, "I am worthless.", have him/her now say, "I have self-worth." or "I am a worthy person." His/her arm will now weaken.

Therapy localize to the various test points (See Figure 8a) (after the person states the "positive' opposite of the negative life belief) to determine which abolishes the weakness. The treatment points for that test point are located on the treatment chart (See Figure 8b).

Treat by having the person tap the treatment point while thinking of the positive life belief (the one which made him/her weak) until he/she is strong after restating the positive statement. In many instances this is enough to eliminate the negative life belief; however, in resistant cases some individuals become psychologically reversed.

Have the person tap the psychological reversal point saying, "I deeply accept myself even though I am or believe I am_____," inserting the negative belief in the blank.

Immediately after, have the person tap the treatment points while thinking of the positive life belief until they remain strong when stating the positive statement and become weak when stating the negative life belief.

Another adjunct to the tapping procedure is to determine which of the flower remedies will be helpful. See Chapter 14, Flower Remedies, for the testing and treating procedure.

One of the most common negative life beliefs is that of being undeserving. There are many individuals who feel that they do not deserve happiness, a good life, success, money, good health, to get completely well - the list goes on and on.

At a seminar in November of 1989, I met Dr. Rob Maddocks, a chiropractic physician from South Carolina. During our discussion about psychological reversal phenomenon, he shared an affirmation he found very helpful in treating peoples' beliefs that they are undeserving.

Here is the affirmation:

I am a perfect child of God.

I am a loving child of God.

I am a deserving child of God.

And I shall have (receive) all the things that I choose or desire that may be beneficial and appropriate for me.

For I am a perfect child of God.

A very loving child of God.

A very deserving child of God.

This affirmation is repeated three times by the person while tapping on the psychological reversal point (See Figures 12a&b) and in some cases, if necessary, (test by therapy localizing) on the heart treatment point on the medial side of the end of the little finger (See Figure 14).

Figure 14

Recently, I was asked to sit in on a group therapy for individuals that were addicted to either alcohol or drugs; I volunteered to assist anyone who would like to use my services in the group. When one alcoholic woman said that she wanted to overcome her addiction to alcohol, she tested strong.

But when she said, "I will not drink any more." she tested weak. That reversal was corrected, and from some remarks she had made while introducing herself, I felt that she had a problem with deserving happiness.

I asked her to say, "I deserve happiness." On testing, she became weak. I then had her repeat the deserving affirmation, and she was immediately cured of her feeling that she did not deserve happiness.

There can be varying degrees of feeling undeserving. For instance, some individuals feel that they deserve to earn, say, thirty thousand dollars a year, but not thirty one thousand or any more! They have set a limit subconsciously, which until treated, will forever keep them from earning more than that amount. They may exceed it at times, but they will subtly or grossly do something to cause their earnings to drop to the fixed amount in their subconscious mind. This was true of a man who was in the same therapy group I mentioned in the previous paragraph. After testing him with the deserving affirmation, he had a new realization that he could earn over one hundred thousand dollars a year!

Occasionally, you will find a person who cannot read or repeat the affirmation. This is due to several deeper negative life beliefs.

One of my patients could not say, "I am a *perfect* child of God." This 36 year old-man believed that he was not a perfect child of God; we had to deal with this first.

We treated his problem by having him think, " I am a *perfect* child of God," and testing him. When he weakened, I had him therapy localize to the various test points. He found the one that abolished the weakness, and then he tapped the corresponding treatment point while he continued to think, "I am a perfect child of God" - until the thought no longer weakened him. At this point he could say, "I am a perfect child of God" -- and accept it.

Another patient could not say, "The things *I* choose...." This gracious, caring and devout 67 year old women believed that she could not choose, only God could choose. Her negative life belief was that she didn't deserve to get completely well, for she could not make that choice. In her case we simply changed the affirmation to "...the things God chooses that may be beneficial...".

To say it the other way caused her anxiety. By changing a few words, we made her feel very comfortable without changing the intent of the affirmation.

Many people have the "Popeye" syndrome. "I am what I am and that's what I am." They believe that they can't be changed, so they cop-out by saying, "I'm just this way."

With the right teacher and the use of these methods, these individuals can release themselves from the bleak sentence of a seemingly unchangeable problem.

Negative life beliefs can affect any facet of life whether it be in recovering health or achieving the spiritual, material or personal goals in our lives.

There are numerous self-help books on the market. There is a list of my favorites in Recommended Reading. One of the best, which I have previously quoted from, is <u>Awaken The Giant Within</u> by Anthony Robbins. He includes a chapter on "Belief Systems," followed by one entitled, "Can Change Happen in an Instant?" Change can happen in an instant he says, provided our beliefs and conviction are strong enough. Corinthians 15:51 says, "Behold, I show you a mystery; We shall not all sleep, but we shall all be changed in a moment, in the twinkling of an eye..."

But if our negative beliefs are subconscious, not recognized, all this "positive" thinking will be as futile as trying to hold back the tides.

Robbins states three qualifying beliefs we must possess to make changes in ourselves. First we must believe, not just that "Something should change" but that it *must* change; this is discussed in Chapter 8 in the various degrees of psychological reversal. In this instance it is the difference between "I will..." and "I want to...".

Second we must believe that " I must change it." This can't be accomplished if a person has a negative life belief that he/she is helpless. And third that "I can change." This can only be achieved if the person believes that he/she is capable.

He goes on to say that without these core beliefs, any changes made stand a good chance of being only temporary.

By determining our exact negative life beliefs, as described previously in this chapter, we have the ability to balance the energies of the body to remove and overcome those beliefs "in the twinkling of an eye."

While the correction usually lasts a long time, in some cases it may need to be checked for and treated again -- particularly if it appears the individual is backsliding. This occurs if the belief is deeply embedded or the authoritative source is continuing to convey the message.

Charles Swindoll wrote a short essay entitled "Attitude." In it he says, "The longer I live, I realize the impact of attitude on life. Attitude, to me, is more important than facts. It is more important than the past, than education, than money, than circumstances, than failures, than successes, than what other people think or say or do. It is more important than appearance, giftedness or skill. It will make or break a company...a church...a home. The remarkable thing is we have a choice every day regarding the attitude we will embrace for that day. We cannot change our past...we cannot change the fact that people will act in a certain way. We cannot change the inevitable. The only thing we can do is play on the one string we have, and that is our attitude...I am convinced that life is 10% what happens to me and 90% how I react to it. And so it is with you...We are in charge of our ATTITUDES."

Vernon Howard, founder of New Life Foundation, Boulder City, NV, said, "The problem is not the first thought but what we think about the thought." By balancing the energies of the body when a person is disturbed by an event, issue, belief or situation, that person can be transformed from the anxiety mode to the problem solving or acceptance mode, and get on with his/her life and be free at last.

It is important to give the person responsibility by teaching him/her how to correct these negative life beliefs (attitudes) and to instruct them on how to do this themselves.

"As he thinketh in his heart, so is he".
- Proverbs 23:7

Chapter 12

Resolving Life Issues

Like negative life beliefs, unresolved life issues can be barriers to happiness, success and fulfillment. While these issues are sometimes a direct part of phobias, anxieties and addictions, they are many times underlying factors contributing to the total problem of the individual.

The most common issues as originally compiled by Dr. Terry Franks are:

power
trust/ing
worthiness
value/ing
self-worth
commitment
freedom
responsibility
forgiveness
faith
boundaries
receiving
allowing
harmony
will
security

claiming
love
peace
joy
compassion
innocence
equality
caring
appreciation
acceptance
oneness
perseverance
releasing
judgement
balance
courage
choosing
connectedness
blame/ing
recognition
rejection

You may be able to think of additional issues which a person may have; if so, add them to the list.

To determine which issue or issues are unresolved with an individual, start with a strong test arm and have the person think of each issue as you read them from your list. In this case, any issue which is bothering the person will make the arm weak. Record the unresolved issue(s).

As always, first determine if the person is psychologically reversed on resolving the issue. Test the person on all the degrees of psychological reversal: I want, I will, I will allow, I deserve to, etc., and correct if necessary (See Chapter 9).

To treat, have the person quantify the intensity of each issue on a scale of '1' to '10' as you have before. Now find the test point which abolishes the weakness for each issue (See Figure 8a) and have the person tap on the corresponding treatment point (See Figure 8b). The quantifying number should drop one or two points after fifteen seconds of tapping. If not, the person is psychologically reversed or the correct treatment point has not been found.

If the person is psychologically reversed, treat as described in Chapter 9. Have the person continue the treatment until the issue reaches '1' (completely gone) or until progress stops. If it stops, check for a mini-psychological reversal; if present, treat and continue. If not present, start the Brain Balancing nine step treatment (Chapter 10). If the issue has not reached '1', continue by tapping on the original treatment point. If the issue still remains, check for further mini-psychological reversals and treat if necessary. If none are present, recheck the original test point to see if it still abolishes the weakness when the person thinks of the issue. If not, have the person therapy localize the other test points to determine where it has shifted -- then tap the new treatment point until the issue is resolved.

As with any other problem, you can test the necessity for the use of Flower remedies for follow-up treatment (See Chapter 14).

Chapter 13

Phobias

A phobia is an unrealistic fear. A phobia is an irrational fear or dread. A phobia is an irrational, excessive and persistent fear of some thing or situation. These dictionary definitions sound less than threatening.

Some others define "phobia" as false evidence appearing real.

Roger Callahan, Ph.D., defines a phobia as a "persistent, irrational fear that causes discomfort." Individuals who suffer from one or more phobias realize that they are very real and have the capacity to cause from mild to severe discomfort, panic or terror. In fact, phobias can completely control one's life.

Phobias can cause reactions such as timidity, apprehension, mistrust, suspicion, qualm, trepidation, nervousness, restlessness, dread, terror, panic and alarm -- all of which can occur in varying degrees of seriousness.

Phobic individuals know their behavior and fears are irrational, but they can't seem to do anything about them. The person's embarrassment and shame about their lack of control leads to further entrenchment of the phobia. This eventually leads to a vicious cycle through which the phobia increases its control.

Like real fears, phobias produce physiological reactions, such as increased heart rate, high blood pressure, rapid breathing (particularly of the shallow chest type), sweaty hands and tightness of neck and back muscles. The irrational nature of phobias causes symptoms that are disproportionate to the event that triggered them and many times prevents the individual from taking steps to resolve the problem.

For example, a person can't enjoy the companionship of a cat or a dog because of his/her irrational fear of these normally friendly pets, and is therefore deprived of the enjoyment that others find in such companionship.

Dr. Robert L. DuPont, director of Washington's Center for Behavior Medicine, describes phobias as "the malignant disease of the 'what-if's'" (Callahan).

Many things can bring on the irrational fear of phobias. The sight of something, a thought, a person, a memory, a situation or an emotional state -- these simple things wreak havoc on some peoples' emotions. Some people are afraid to get emotionally close to anyone, therefore they never fall in love for fear of being rejected. Fear of rejection is probably the most universal fear, and it accounts for more of life's failures than any other fear. Other phobias include fear of animals, insects, rodents, snakes, heights, dentists, shopping, getting up to speak in front of a group, flying, elevators, freeways, bridges, success, failure - the list goes on and on. (See Appendix).

Anything, anybody or any situation can bring on an irrational state of fear.

Some people have many phobias and some have only one. As previously mentioned in Chapter 3, this author had a phobia regarding anything touching his eyes -- or anybody's eyes, for that matter. I could not watch anyone put in or remove their contact lenses. The thought of getting contact lenses was unthinkable. I would not allow an eye doctor to preform a glaucoma test, even though anesthetic drops were to be used. I never had an eye injury that explained the phobia. I finally decided to treat myself, and was completely cured in just ten minutes! Soon after that I went for an eye examination and allowed the doctor to do the glaucoma test. I was completely relaxed through the procedure.

Many people never bother seeking help for their phobias because their irrational fears do not actually interfere with their lifestyle -- or at least they rationalize this. After all, you can get from Phoenix to Miami by bus or train and not have to fly; it just takes a little longer. A neighbor of mine, who is afraid of flying, was scheduled to go on a Caribbean cruise. She lives in Arizona and rode the bus for three days to Miami because of her fear. I offered to treat her, but she replied she had plenty of time and "liked to see the countryside." She was so phobic about flying that she was afraid to be treated because she feared she would be cured and have to fly. In her irrationality, she could not imagine being free of the fear.

This type of fear was proclaimed by president Franklin D. Roosevelt in his 1933 Inaugural Address when he said, "The only thing we have to fear is fear itself." A "Dear Abby" column went on to reveal that Roosevelt was not the first to express this idea. Paraphrasing Ms. Van Buren, she told her readers that "The Duke of Wellington, according to the Earl of Stanhope in his Notes of Conversations with the Duke of Wellington (1888) said, 'The only thing I am afraid of is fear'."

"Wellington may have gotten the idea from Thoreau who said, "Nothing is so much to be feared as fear." in his Journal of 1851.

"Thoreau was not the first to voice this idea as he may have gotten it from Francis Bacon who wrote in De Augmentis Scientiarum, Book II, Fortitudo, 1623, "Nothing is terrible except fear itself."

"Possibly Thoreau read Essays' Book I (1580) by Michel Montaigne in which he wrote, "The thing I fear most is fear."

"Perhaps The Old Testament gives us wise direction by admonishing us to, "Be not afraid of sudden fear."

Good advice, but up until the discoveries of Callahan this was but a very nice academic proclamation. Throughout this book you will learn to quickly and effectively conquer fear in yourself and others.

It is estimated that one out of every nine people have a significant phobia. By significant, I mean one that actually causes enough discomfort that it can't be ignored. There are many mild phobias, disguised fears and compulsive behaviors that are rooted in fears, which are not included in this total (Callahan). The health community is becoming increasingly aware of the role of psychobiology and the mind-body connection. Only the uninformed or those doctors who are unwilling to look with eyes that see still separate the body and mind.

Whenever we remember, think, see, taste, smell, hear or touch anything, it is registered in the lower limbic system of the brain and often in the cerebral cortex. Depending on the threat and intensity of whatever it was, impulses are directed to the hypothalamus and subsequently to the pituitary and the autonomic nervous system so the appropriate action can be taken by the individual.

Callahan discovered and developed the first effective rapid treatment of phobias after attending a basic seminar in applied kinesiology. After learning about the meridian system (acupuncture), and each of the twelve energy meridians representing a specific emotion, he hypothesized that the body had a psychological immune system just as it has a physical immune system. Furthermore, if any of these energy meridians were not in balance, the psychological immune system could not handle negative emotions in a normal manner. Since a phobia, which is an unrealistic fear, can't be differentiated from a real fear by the primitive portion of the brain -- the hypothalamus -- the body reacts as if the fear is real, and depending on the intensity of the problem, takes the appropriate physical steps for survival: increased blood pressure, heart rate, breathing, etc.

Callahan further hypothesized that if there was an imbalance in the meridian system, the body would not remain in the problem solving mode, but instead would go into the anxiety mode, with all the symptoms of the phobic reaction. He then found that by tapping the beginning or end of the energy meridian that was out of balance, while the patient was thinking of the fear, the body would switch from the anxiety mode to the problem solving mode and the physical preparation for fight or flight would be stopped. This resulted from the body's psychological immune system being normalized. In addition, he found that generally, the balancing of the meridian while the patient was thinking of the specific phobia would be very long lasting, if not permanent. In his book, Five Minute Phobia Cure, he says that he does not know how this happens -- but that it does. He compares this with the use of electricity. Scientists know that it works but can't fully explain how it works -- but that does not stop us from using it.

There are some real fears, however, which are meant to protect us from injury. These fears allow us to take the proper precautions to prevent injury or even death. The fear that we might be injured in an auto accident prompts us to buckle up when we get in a car and to follow traffic laws. The fear of drowning prompts us to be sure that we wear a life preserver or have one easily accessible when riding in a boat. The fear of being hit by a car or truck while crossing a street prompts us to look both ways before crossing. These are positive fears and help us stay alive.

While there are many real fears that are meant to protect us from injury, the majority of our fears are irrational fears, or phobias, which can be described as "False Expectations/Education, Appearing Real." They prevent us from enjoying a drive across a beautiful bridge, through the scenic mountains, along the freeway. They keep us from flying across the nation in a few hours rather than taking a four to five day journey in a car. They prevent us from going on a hike because we might see a spider or a snake. They prevent us from getting the proper health care because of the fear of various examination procedures. They prevent us from meeting new people, lovers, business prospects. The list goes on and on.

It is the irrational fear that the treatment taught in this book eliminates. It takes away all the irrationality and retains the common sense to look both ways before crossing the street, to respect potentially dangerous things, places or situations.

Most people think of "crippled" people as those who have lost the use of some part of the body or have actually lost some part of the body through injury or disease. We can conjure up all kinds of images of individuals in wheel chairs, on crutches, using artificial limbs, limping along as they attempt to walk, unable to climb stairs, bedridden - the images are many.

However, the worst crippling is not physical but psychological. While some physically crippled people are psychologically crippled because of their physical condition and their attitude toward their bodies, millions of others have a different problem. These others, millions of whom are very physically fit (in fact, some who are world class athletes) are just as crippled from unrealistic fears (phobias) anxieties, compulsive behaviors, addictions to various substances (food, tobacco, alcohol or drugs) love pain, post traumatic syndromes, self-limiting or self-destructive negative life beliefs, etc.

These individuals have figuratively placed themselves in a prison from which there seems no escape. I say "seems" because their fear is occasionally so severe that even the thought of facing the problem is overwhelming and thus crippling. In some instances, an individual is strong enough to seek professional help, although prior to this revolutionary new treatment procedure, they had to endure a long and sometimes painful process to overcome the problem.

The two major motivating forces in our lives are pain and pleasure. Depending on each individual, either or both can be a driving force. In the instance of phobias, anxieties, addictions, compulsive behavior and or post traumatic stress syndrome, the feeling that motivates the individual to do something about it is either pain or pleasure. If the pain is such that the person can't stand it anymore, the individual will be motivated to seek treatment to gain the pleasure of being free from the problem. Conversely, if the pain is great but not great enough, the fear of actually having to face the problem keeps many from seeking treatment. Individuals in this state usually can't be treated successfully because of the phenomenon, psychological reversal.

There are many books and self-help tapes that address the problem. One such book, Feel the Fear...and Do It Anyway by Susan Jeffers, Ph.D., is an excellent program for many, but it assumes that individuals are able to come up with the strength to begin. In some cases that may be true. Dr. Jeffers has many techniques to get a person off of square one. But for the individual who has a true phobia, however, the fear is usually so great that he/she will not even attempt to take action. One will not even attempt to feel the fear because the pain which it brings is overwhelming.

Dr. Jeffers classifies fears in three levels.

Level 1: Includes fears of those things that do happen to us such as aging, dying, war, retirement, accidents and rape; also, fears that require action, such as making decisions, changing a career, losing weight, public speaking, intimacy and making a mistake.

Her level 2 fears have to do with inner state of mind such as rejection, success, failure, helplessness.

Her level 3 is simply, "I can't handle it!"

Level 1 translates into, "I can't handle what life brings me; I can't handle aging, illness, losing my job, being alone, losing him/her, losing my money, etc."

Level 2 translates into, "I can't handle success, failure, being rejected, etc."

Level 3 translates into, "I can't handle anything." This includes the problems of level 1 and level 2, plus the other phobias that one may have, such as fear of cats, dogs, heights, flying, snakes, spiders, dentists, doctors, needles, etc., and the complex phobia of agoraphobia.

In the book Phobia: A Comprehensive Summary of Modern Treatments edited by Robert L DuPont, M.D., Robert M. Doctor reports, "In summary, we can say that while psychiatrists, physicians and psychologists were significantly less effective than counselors and other procedures, no type of profession demonstrated clear effectiveness in treating agoraphobia. This was particularly evident with physicians where their drug-oriented approach was highly unsuccessful. Psychiatrists and psychologists, who were presumably trained in treatment of such disorders, were also clearly unsuccessful. Furthermore, psychiatrists persisted with treatment for a significantly longer period of time than the other professions yet yielded inferior treatment results.

"Based on these results and the presumed base-rate for spontaneous remission (2,3,4,) traditional psychotherapies and drugs are not adequate forms of treatment for agoraphobia." (Italics added.)

Agoraphobia is commonly defined as a fear of the market place or open spaces. It is a collection of many different phobias. Most agoraphobiacs are unable to leave their homes for more than a few minutes or hours -- and some, not at all. If they are able to leave their homes, they are usually under a great degree of anxiety, sometimes to the point of panic while away from home.

Fortunately there is a way to handle agoraphobia and all fears -- by balancing the energies in the body with a very simple stimulation of specific acupuncture points. This stimulation is done by tapping on these points for about fifteen seconds and monitoring the decrease in the fear.

For the treatment of all phobias, use the procedures described in Chapter 10.

Chapter 14

Flowers

As previously mentioned in Chapter 9, the use of Bach Flower Remedies, particularly Rescue Remedy, has proven very helpful for psychological reversal. I found that the Bach Flower Remedies and other flower remedies could also be used to assist in the treatment of phobias, self limiting and negative life beliefs many patients have.

Dr. Edward Bach was a respected homeopathic physician in London during the 1920's, and until his death in 1936. Before becoming interested in homeopathy he was an orthodox medical physician specializing in bacteriology. He observed that patients carrying specific bacterial pathogens had specific personality temperaments. First, he treated them with homeopathic remedies. Not liking to give nosodes (a homeopathic remedy prepared from disease producing agents such as bacteria or other micro-organisms) he began his search for natural agents that would deal with specific personalities; and he found these agents in flowers.

He discovered an illness-personality link that subtly affects the body by lowering its natural resistance -- eventually causing illness. He reasoned that if the emotional factors could be corrected, the physical disease could be cured. Bach had a very sensitive psychic ability. While walking in the countryside touching the dew from the flowers, he felt all of the physical and emotional symptoms to which the flowers' essence were an antidote. To prepare the various essences, he gathered specific flowers, placed them in containers of pure spring water, and then let them sit in the sun for several hours. Afterwards he created a homeopathic preparation from the flower treated water.

Bach found that specific flowers relieved specific emotional symptoms, and he eventually classified thirty eight different flowers according to their effects. He combined five into what he called Rescue Remedy. Rescue Remedy seems to work very well for anyone who has experienced a physical accident or emotional trauma (Gerber). (Bach Flower Remedies can be ordered from Ellon Bach, U.S.A., Inc., 644 Merrick Rd., Lynbrook, NY 11563, Telephone 1-800-433-7523)

In 1984, while taking advanced seminars taught by Terry Franks, D.C. of Burnsville, Minnesota, I was introduced to two other groups of flower remedies: the Flower Essences - commonly called the "California Flower Remedies" developed by Richard Katz in 1979 and produced by Flower Essence Society, P.O. Box 459, Nevada City, CA 95959. Telephone 1-800 548-0075; the Petite Fluer Essence - commonly called the Texas Remedies produced by Judy Ermis, N.D., Ph.D., 5414 Bellaire, Suite 333, Bellaire, TX 77401, Telephone 713-665-2290; and Living Flower Essences, P.O. Box 1492, Cottonwood, AZ 86326.

These flower remedies are made in the same manner of the Bach Remedies, but are composed of a wider variety of flowers that address many more facets of the basic emotions.

These new remedies seem to assist with the processes of inner growth and spiritual awakening. They aid in removing blockages such as fears about sexuality, issues of intimacy, sensitivity (Gerber).

The diagnosis for the need of the various remedies was done originally on a symptomatic and empirical basis, which most of the time seemed to have a good degree of success.

In the early 1960's, Deutsch discovered that various substances have an effect on the strength of an individual. He related to me that he was having a rodent problem in his home and had purchased a box of poison. One of his young daughters wanted to help him carry the items he had purchased into the house. He gave her the one pound box of the rodent poison and on the way in she complained of the heaviness of the bag. He thought that was strange and after entering the house he then gave her a one pound bag of pop corn which she did not find "heavy." He asked her which was heavier and she said the bag she had carried into the house.

He wondered why she would find the box of rodent poison heavy, but soon put it out of his mind until about a year later when he attended a muscle testing seminar taught by Goodheart. When Goodheart was demonstrating the relationship of nutrition and muscle strength, Deutsch remembered the incident about his daughter and the rodent poison. When he arrived home he put a small amount of the rodent poison in a plastic bag and had his daughter hold the sealed bag; when he tested her arm muscle, it weakened.

Deutsch applied this new finding to his clinical practice and found that the electromagnetic field of the body could be influenced in a positive or negative manner. If a toxic substance was placed against the body, a strong muscle would weaken. Conversely, if there was a weak muscle and the correct nutritional supplement was placed in the body's electromagnetic field, the weak muscle would strengthen.

Deutsch introduced me to this new way of testing to determine the need for remedies, or whether a specific substance would have an adverse effect on an individual. This method involved the interplay of electromagnetic fields or vibrations. Gerber, in his book <u>Vibrational Medicine</u>, discusses these subtle energies and their effect on the body. This method has not as yet been scientifically researched and is not an authorized procedure of the International College of Applied Kinesiology. It has been and is being clinically researched by numerous doctors of a number of disciplines.

Testing for a flower remedy consists of first having the person think of his/her phobia or anxiety or make the statement that causes weakness (Goodheart). Next, the bottle of whatever flower remedy is to be tested is placed on the body of the person, observing if there is a change in the strength of the person's indicator muscle.

There are a number of very delicate instruments available to measure the extremely weak electrical currents that are changed by introducing substances into the energy field of an individual, such as the Vega, the Voll and the Entero. These instruments, however, are very expensive and are available only to doctors. The discoveries of Goodheart and Deutsch make it possible to use manual muscle testing in their place.

Because there are thirty eight Bach Remedies, sixty Petite Fluer Remedies and seventy two Flower Essence Remedies, it appeared that the testing might be very laborious. Franks found that approximately thirty of the remedies could be tested simultaneously. That is, a box of thirty test bottles could be laid on the person while he/she was thinking of a specific thought or making a specific statement that weakened the indicator muscle. If there was no increase in the muscle strength, there was nothing in the box that would be helpful. Conversely, if there was a strengthening of the indicator muscle, it indicated that there was one or more bottles in that particular box that would be effective.

To determine which specific remedy (or remedies) is effective, the box would then be removed from the person's body and then the person places one hand over half the bottles in the box while thinking or saying the same thing. If that does not strengthen the indicator muscle, the other side would be halved again and the person touches one of the halves to see if there is a strengthening. This continues until one or more test bottles are found to be effective. In most cases, the body is so specific that only one test bottle will strengthen the indicator muscle. Using this method, the person's body is selecting the precise remedy for its needs at that time.

To make the remedy, follow the directions which come with the remedies. The Bach Remedies suggest that in a one ounce amber colored dropper capped bottle, put in one tenth of an ounce of brandy (used as a preservative). To this, fill the rest of the bottle with pure water such as spring or filtered, but not tap or distilled water. Add three to four drops of undiluted stock remedy to the brandy water mixture you have prepared. It is then necessary to succuss (vigorously shaking) the dropper capped bottle by striking it sharply on the palm of your hand one hundred times. As an alternative to brandy, you can use ten drops of ethyl alcohol (as a preservative) in one ounce of water. The ethyl alcohol can be purchased in most liquor stores as a product called Ever Clear which is 190 proof ethyl alcohol. For those who's religion or personal beliefs demand complete abstinence from alcohol, the brandy or ethyl alcohol may be omitted, but the bottle must be kept refrigerated.

The usual dosage of flower remedies is five drops of the diluted mixture, three times a day. Instruct the person to drop the liquid in the mouth, preferably under the tongue, without the dropper touching the mouth or tongue. The remedy should be held in the mouth for one minute before swallowing to allow for sublingual absorption. It should also be taken at least thirty minutes before or after eating or brushing one's teeth.

Sometimes the flower remedies act very quickly such as in the use of rescue remedy; however, most of the time the effects are gradual and subtle. There are rarely any side effects unless there is a deeper problem that was not determined or addressed. In such cases, the usual effect is that of depression or anxiety. The individual you are working with will usually tell you about it as it happens. If this does occur, you need to do some deductive detective work starting from the general to the specific.

Walker, in his work known as Neuro Emotional Technic, offers an excellent procedure to narrow down the area of concern. He explains to the person that there are two basic things in life: money, which includes finances, career and job; and love, which includes everyone whom you have ever loved or who has loved you. The type of love can be romantic or platonic.

To use this method, explain that the original drops cleared one layer of the problem. But, in clearing it, uncovered something deeper and brought the suppressed depression or anxiety to the surface. Ask if he/she would like to discover the cause of the newly surfaced problem. After receiving permission you may proceed with the deductive technique.

Explain to the person that there are two things in life, money and love as explained above. Have the person think of each one separately and test a strong muscle after each thought. Either the money or love thought will weaken the strong muscle. As an illustration, let's say that the thought of love weakened the muscle. The next step is to make the statement to the person you are working with, that the individual who is involved can be either male or female. Have the person think of one at a time, that is, male or female and test. Whichever weakens is the correct gender. Let's say it was female. There are two types of female, family or friends. If family weakens, there are two types of family, immediate - mother, sisters and daughters or extended, such as grandmothers, aunts, nieces and cousins. You can see that as you break this down, you soon come to a specific individual. You may then test the various test points to find which one abolishes the weakness.

If it was friends and not family, there are two types of love involved, platonic and romantic. Once this is determined a name can usually be found. Sometimes, in order to determine the person and the incident, it may be necessary to determine the year in which the incident occurred. This can be done by scanning backward from the present. For instance, if the person you are treating is age 45, have him/her think of age 40-45 and test. If this is not the age bracket in which the incident occurred, there will not be any change in strength; if it is, there will be. Proceed backwards until a five year bracket is found, then go through the individual years in that bracket until the correct age is found. In some instances you might find that the incident happened in utero. I watched Dr. Walker testing a patient who was unable to make any lasting commitments to anyone and it was found that he had a twin who died in utero. This had a profound effect which prevented him from making a commitment for fear of being hurt again!

Now that you have helped the person find the source of the pain, find the new flower remedy which also abolishes the weakness, and give this for follow-up treatment after the appropriate tapping treatment is completed. To do this, have the person locate the acupuncture test point which abolishes the weakness and tap the treatment point associated with that test point while thinking of the individual until thinking of the individual no longer makes the person weak. For more information about doctors who use Walker's Neuro Emotional Technic in your area, you can contact him at: 500 2nd St., Encinitas, CA 92024. Telephone (619) 753-1533. Only doctors licensed to diagnose and their assistants are allowed to take Walker's seminars. For information on seminars call 1-800-888-4638.

Flowers are a subtle but very powerful remedy.

Chapter 15

Addiction to Food

Addiction to food is the most ubiquitous of all addictions; food is necessary for life. We can't abstain from food.

Eating is not only necessary for survival, but it has become a key part of our social life. We eat at celebrations of happiness and success, at holidays, birthdays and anniversaries. We also eat in times of disappointments, depression, sorrow, loss and grief -- when it comforts us.

When we are invited by friends or family to their homes, one of the first things they say is, "Would you like something to eat? Have a piece of pie, cake, a sandwich, candy, ice cream, etc." And if we decline, especially if they have gone to the trouble of preparing something special they feel rejected and we feel guilty for not accepting their hospitality. On the other hand, when we invite others to visit us, we offer our guests the same and they feel an obligation to eat something to show us that they appreciate our thoughtfulness.

We eat when we're glad and we eat when we're sad -- especially when we are sad! Dean Ornish, M.D. in his book Eat More and Weight Less states, "We give food the power to make us happy or sad and in some cases, even to control our lives." He goes further in saying that if we have pain and or emptiness, we begin to look in all the wrong places to fill this emptiness and kill the pain with food, alcohol, cigarettes, overwork and so forth.

Callahan has written a book entitled, <u>Why Do I Eat When I'm Not Hungry?</u> Janet Greeson, Ph.D. has written a book entitled, <u>It's Not What You Eat, It's What's Eating You!</u> Both of these books convey the idea that when we are under stress, anxiety, depression or any other form of emotional tension, we look for ways to relieve the pain. For many of us it is food.

In 1993, Sally Jessy Raphael featured three women on her popular talk show who had substituted food for sex. Because of their overeating, the women's bodies and their relationships with their spouses suffered. One woman's husband denied her sex because of her appearance. Because of this, she ate more and more and the vicious cycle continued. Another woman's husband divorced her. The third woman refused to have sex with her husband because she felt so unattractive she couldn't see why her husband could still want her -- although he continually reassured her that he did.

It was obvious the issue was not sex, but the women's feelings about themselves. One had been abused as a child and had been "date-raped" three times. She had literally built a wall of fat to protect herself from others. The second woman's posture, even while sitting, was cowering -- very indicative of someone who was in a protective stance. Even when asked to stand up, she never did stand up fully, but resumed her protective stance. The third woman was 162 pounds when she married, and carried it well on her 6'1'' frame. However, she had since gained two hundred pounds, and had such a low self esteem that she refused to have sex with her husband, even though he repeatedly told her that her size didn't matter. Since she denied herself (as well as her husband) she made up for it by eating more -- although she knew this would make her even more self-conscious and unworthy of his attention.

A fourth guest, Geneen Roth, wrote the book, <u>When Food is Love</u>. This book's message was that some individuals substitute food for love and/or sex. The book went on to explain that dieting always ends up with weight gain if the basic issue of self worth is not addressed and resolved. She also said that people equate self worth with body size. That is, they feel, "If I were thin I would feel better about myself." She emphasized that one's self worth must come first, and this will naturally lead to a comfortable body size.

In her book, Roth states that for every diet there is an equal and opposite binge. Therefore, eat what you want and stop when you are full. In other words, don't deny yourself, but don't ever overeat! Easy to say, but difficult - if not impossible - to do if you are eating to satisfy an emotional void.

Food brings many of us the feeling of pleasure or love or satisfaction. Except for the masochistic, we prefer pleasure over pain, love over emptiness and satisfaction over an emotional void. In fact, if we have even the slightest pain, we look for a way to alleviate it. Drug companies know this; that is why there are so many ads for pain killers. We hear the message all the time: "Don't cope, take dope" (aspirin, Tylenol, Alka-Seltzer, Advil, Motrin, Valium, etc.). "Relief is just a swallow away." For anxieties and emotional pain, the quickest and most accessible tranquilizer is food. Eating is pleasing to our taste; a full belly comforts us. How often have we heard someone say, "Come on, have something to eat, it will make you feel better."

I am reminded of a cartoon illustrating a person looking in an open refrigerator laden with food. The caption said, "Looking for love in the wrong places."

Even if we are not prompted by someone, we remember how food comforted us in the past when we were troubled. For instance, if our parents were fighting and we felt stressed, we may have gone to grandma's house, where she always comforted us with pot roast, mashed potatoes and gravy, setting up a conditioned reflex. As adults we immediately go for the same heavy, high calorie, fat-laden comfort we remember. After all, didn't food remove all the tension and anxiety before?

Some of us may have been sent to the candy store as a way to get us out of the house. As a result, we learned that chocolate or other sweets would take away the hurt. The list goes on and on as to what, as children, we may have learned to use as our tranquilizers.

As mentioned in Chapter 3, I used food as one of my tranquilizers. As a side effect, I gained weight until I topped the scale at 193 pounds in 1985! My trouble began soon after I was married the first time. Within five years, I had gone from a trim 140 pounds to a pudgy 182 pounds. I lost the weight, only to gain it back again. I played the yo-yo game for many years before finally discovering why I continually gained it all back and then some. To this day, I still tend to use food as my tranquilizer, and I must constantly balance my energies when under stress, so I do not fall back into the same situation.

There are many reasons why a person uses food as a tranquilizer or builds up fat mass as protection. Fortunately, with Acu-POWER, the cause of the problem can be diagnosed and the proper treatment can be given. The majority of people who are overweight are psychologically reversed regarding their weight. The reason for this is generally due to a negative life belief (See Chapter 11), or post traumatic stress syndrome that will be discussed in Chapter 19.

To treat for food addiction, first determine if there is psychological reversal (See Chapter 9) regarding weight loss before beginning treatment on the actual addictive urge for food. If a person is psychologically reversed regarding weight loss, he/she will weaken when the indicator muscle is tested when making the statement, "I want to lose weight." and will stay strong when saying, "I want to gain weight!"

In most cases, it will surprise the person that he/she subconsciously wants to gain weight rather than lose weight! For this reason, you must tactfully discuss the possibility of psychological reversal before testing for it. It is best to ask the person if he/she wonders why it has not been possible to lose any weight, or why when he/she loses some, gains it right back and possibly even more. After the person responds, ask permission to perform a test that will show whether or not what he/she is saying is really what he/she believes subconsciously. Be sure to emphasize that the belief is subconscious.

After obtaining permission, proceed with the psychological reversal testing. Ask the person how many pounds he/she wants to lose. Instruct the person to say, "I want to lose____pounds" (the number he/she has just given you) and test the strong arm (See Figure 6b). If it stays strong it means the person wants to lose that number of pounds. If the arm weakens (See Figure 6c), it means that he/she is psychologically reversed and must be treated for that first. In some cases the person will test strong for "I want to" but when asked to say, "I will do all the things necessary to lose____pounds," will weaken. This means that the psychological reversal runs deeper; treat it in the same way as the previous psychological reversal, but use a different affirmation.

In the first scenario, "I want", the affirmation is "I deeply accept myself even though I don't want to lose____ pounds." As an alternative, the affirmation could be, "I deeply accept myself, even though I am overweight." In the second case, "I will", the affirmation is, "I deeply accept myself even if I NEVER lose ____pounds." These affirmations are repeated at least three times while tapping on the psychological reversal point (See Figures 12 a&b).

After treating the psychological reversal, have the person think of his/her favorite food and rate his/her desire or urge to eat it on a scale of one to ten (ten being highest, meaning he/she must have it now and can't turn it down; and one meaning that he/she has no desire at all).

To show the person he/she is accurate on the quantifying evaluation, have him/her state the number he/she has determined to be the correct evaluation and test a strong arm. If it remains strong, that is the correct number. If not, ask the person to say one number above or below the original number, and test until you find the correct number. Usually the person is not more than one point off. If he/she can not give a number it means that he/she is not in very close touch with his/her feelings. In that case, the number can be determined by a muscle test starting from ten and counting backwards until you reach a number causing the arm to stay strong.

While he/she is thinking of the food, test a strong arm. It should weaken. If not, that food is not a problem, or possibly the person is neurologically disorganized. (See Chapter 9 for diagnosis and treatment.) After correcting the neurological disorganization, you are now ready to continue testing. With the opposite hand, have him/her touch test point 1 (See Figure 8b) and retest the arm while the person is thinking of the food and how much he/she would like to eat some. In about 95 percent of cases, the arm will now be strong. If not, have him/her touch test point 2 (See Figure 8b) and repeat the test. In some cases this will not test strong, and then it is just a matter of proceeding through the remaining test points to find the one which abolishes the weakness when thinking of the food.

When the correct test point is found, find the corresponding treatment point (See Figure 8b). To treat, have the person tap the points just under the eyes, as illustrated in Figure 8b, (in the case of strengthening by touching test point 1). If a person strengthens with a point other than test point 1, use the appropriate corresponding treatment point while he/she is thinking of how satisfying and how good it would taste to have whatever food he/she is thinking about. Keep reminding the person to think of how good it would be to have some right now, how satisfying it would be, etc.

After tapping for about 15 seconds, ask the person to quantify his/her desire. It usually will go down at least two points if the desire started above 6. You can test the accuracy of the person's quantifying by testing the strong arm; if it stays strong while he/she says, "I'm at a ___ " the statement is true. If it weakens, the person is probably just one point off. If the person did not go down at least one point, the person is probably psychologically reversed regarding that particular food. To test, have him/her say, "I want to overcome my desire for___". If the arm tests weak there is psychological reversal. To treat, have the person tap on the psychological reversal point (See Figures 12 a&b) saying, "I deeply accept myself even though I have a desire for _____ ". Resume tapping on the original treatment points and the desire will now go down.

Occasionally, if the person started at a six or seven, after encouraging him/her during the initial tapping process to think of how good the food would be, the desire actually increases. This is because he/she was not really concentrating on the food and how much he/she liked it when originally tested. After really concentrating on the food, the desire increases to where it should have been to start with. If this happens, explain what the problem was and have the person continue tapping. After the desire reaches its peak it will decrease.

Sometimes in the reduction process, the person will get stuck at some point. For instance, if he/she reached a four and can't get any lower, it is time to check for a mini-reversal. Have him/her say, "I want to get lower than a four on my desire for _____". If he/she tests weak on this statement have the person repeat three times, "I deeply accept myself even though I can't get lower than a four on my desire for_____", while tapping on the psychological reversal point.

If the person did not have a mini-reversal it is time to proceed to the next step -- Brain Balancing. Have him/her tap on the Brain Balance point on the back of the hand, one half inch behind and between the fourth and fifth knuckles, while thinking of the desire (See Figure 11). Proceed with the Brain Balance nine-step procedure illustrated in Chapter 10. This should reduce the desire to '1'. If not, check for another mini-reversal and treat it if necessary. If not a mini-reversal, have the person continue tapping on the original treatment point. This should bring the desire to a '1'. If not, have the person think of the desire for the food and touch the original test point. If it still strengthens the weakness the corresponding treatment point needs further tapping. If not, proceed to the next test point until one is found that strengthens, and tap the corresponding treatment points.

Ask the person if there is any desire left for the food. If he/she says no, you are finished. You can impress on the person that the desire is really gone by having him/her state, "I have completely and totally released (or lost) all my desire for_____." Test a strong arm. If the statement is true, the arm will remain strong. If it weakens, it means there is still some desire and treatment must continue. In most cases you will find there is another mini-reversal and they are stuck at a '1 1/2' or '1 1/4'. Some people have a hard time completely releasing all their desire because subconsciously, this food is his/her tranquilizer or crutch and he/she is afraid to be without it.

Each food highly desired by the person must be worked through the same process, because each may represent a different anxiety that needs to be dealt with. It may sound like a lot of work, but there is no other method that even comes close to combating the basic underlying cause of the food addiction.

At this point, it would be a good idea to ask the person to try to recall emotionally upsetting times going back to his/her childhood in order to discover what he/she ate to relieve the anxiety. Whatever was eaten, whether it be one or more things, acts as a trigger mechanism. Once it is eaten the individual seems to go into an eating frenzy. In other words, the food eaten as a tranquilizer causes the person to lose control of all discipline regarding eating. It would be best to treat for the desires of these trigger foods first -- it will usually save a lot of time.

Remember, this process is balancing the energies of the body so that the person can cope with the emotional stress that causes the pain he/she tries to alleviate by eating.

For those who eat after they are full, a practice commonly referred to as gluttony, it is necessary to have them treat themselves with the Brain Balancing procedure several times a day. First, check them for psychological reversal regarding eating after they are full, and treat as necessary. Instruct the person to think of eating after he/she has finished their regular meal. Go though the brain balancing procedure until all the desire to stuff themselves is gone. It is important to understand these individuals are finding pleasure in the taste of the food, in hope of blotting out the emotional pain. They will usually suffer a number of mini-reversals in the process, which must be treated as they occur.

In some individuals it may be necessary to search much deeper to find out why he/she is carrying extra weight. The extra weight can be as little as ten pounds or as much as several hundred pounds. Individuals who have been victims of rape, incest, bullying or any other physical abuse will use the extra weight as protection. In cases like this, have the person say, or think, if they are unable to verbalize, "I keep this extra weight for protection." Test the arm - if it remains strong, the statement is true. If not, go for additional statements as to possibilities of why he/she would want to keep extra weight. It can be fear, grief, anger, spite, self esteem, resentment, security or whatever negative emotion or life belief is held by the person. See Chapter 11 and 12 for negative life beliefs and issues.

I had one patient, a 33 year old beautician, who was always twenty pounds overweight. She was a very pretty woman, who in addition to fixing women's hair also cut and styled men's hair. She was always saying that she wanted to lose the twenty pounds, but no matter what diet she attempted, she failed. She related her frustration to me while she was in the office for a neck problem. I tested her for reversal and she was reversed on wanting to lose weight. That was corrected, and we started the regular procedure. This helped temporarily, but she could never lose more than five to seven pounds. Later, during additional testing to find the reason for her continued reversals, she remarked that she thought because one of her male customers had made a pass at her once, if she slimmed down by losing the twenty pounds, more men would make passes at her. She went on to explain that she was very happily married and just didn't want to encourage any more men to make passes at her.

I explained that her fear of men making passes at her could be treated and eliminated, but her fear was too great for her to proceed. She resigned herself to the seeming safety and protection of the twenty pounds.

A possible explanation of her reluctance is that her real fear was not that men would make passes at her, but the fear that a situation would arise in which she might not resist the pass. She was not going to put herself in a position to test herself. We did not pursue the issue, and soon after I moved to my present location in Arizona. This issue may have been followed though and corrected, but time and opportunity passed. This is a delicate subject and if pursued, must be done in a diplomatic and non-threatening way, and certainly with the person's permission.

From this, you can see that many fears, issues, life beliefs and traumas can cause someone to overeat. With the ability to muscle test and find out what the person's real problem is, most people can be successfully treated. This is not the only way that a person can be treated. It is an important tool that can be used independently or in conjunction with other methods to substantially cut treatment time. Acu-POWER treatment can enhance the effectiveness of weight loss programs such as Weight Watchers, Nutri-System, Jenny Craig or any other quality program.

For those trying to lose weight it is important to drink plenty of water every day. How much is plenty? According to their weight, they must drink two-thirds of an ounce of WATER for each pound that they presently weigh, every day. This carries away all the waste products of the body and actually acts as a natural diuretic. (Coffee, tea, fruit juice, milk, pop and alcohol, while fluids, are not water and the body does not metabolize them as such.)

It has been stated by many knowledgeable people in the health and weight loss field that diets don't work. There has to be a distinct life style change. Ornish has found that most individuals will find it easier to make a major life style change than minor ones. I highly recommend that you read his book, <u>Eat More and Weigh Less</u>. You will find that using the Acu-POWER procedures along with his program will be of great assistance to your success.

Exercise is also an assistance, since it not only burns calories, but if done correctly, creates fat-burning enzymes that allow the body to use your body's fat for energy instead of sugar (Covert Bailey). In addition, exercise helps create a sense of well being, reduces anxiety and dissipates depression. The correct exercise to create fat-burning enzymes is aerobic exercise. Unfortunately, most so called aerobic exercise classes bring the heart rate too high, thus making the exercise actually anaerobic. Most individuals will find walking to be an excellent non-traumatic form of exercise. For a more complete discussion I recommend the book Fit or Fat, by Covert Bailey, Ph.D. and Everyone Is An Athlete, by Philip Maffetone, D.C..

While unresolved emotions almost always account for addiction to food, there are other causes. Individuals should be examined for the possibility of Candidia Albicans infection. Function of the endocrine system, particularly the thyroid must be examined and treated. Most people who are allergic to a food, or to certain foods, crave them and fall into a never ending vicious cycle of allergic reaction -- one symptom being added weight in the form of fluid and fat. Often, eliminating this food, even for just a month or two will remove it from the allergic state. Obviously, overcoming the *craving* for a food to which you are allergic is a must; it can be accomplished by the use of Acu-POWER procedures.

Chapter 16

Addiction to Tobacco

Next to food, tobacco, whether smoked or chewed, is the second most common addiction. It causes many debilitating diseases (despite the tobacco industries denials). Every package of cigarettes, cigars and oral tobacco products, must, as mandated by law, carry a warning stating it may be hazardous to the health of the user. Nevertheless, billions of people use tobacco as their tranquilizer of choice. Most get started at an early age because of peer pressure, and soon grow to crave the substance.

Insidiously, psychological dependence sets in. Continued use produces a physical dependence. Unfortunately, most people -- including most doctors -- think the physical dependence should be the primary focus of treatment. Look at all the ads for nicotine replacement products. One of the most popular product is a prescription chewing gum called Nicorette. I had a patient who was spending $70.00-$80.00 per month on this nicotine substitute chewing gum! Her's was a difficult case, but in two one hour treatment sessions, she was completely free of the nicotine addiction. Another popular product is a prescription-only nicotine skin patch that gives you a steady "nicotine fix" while you are wearing it. This method requires a new patch every day, and as the ABC-TV medical advisor Dr. Tim Johnson says, "This type of treatment requires counseling, or it will not be successful in most cases." Everyone is aware of the high cost of counseling and the seemingly endless hours it takes. The counseling, of course, is needed to treat the psychological addiction.

The fact is, physical addiction can be overcome in 48 to 72 hours! That's right, it takes only 48 to 72 hours for the body to completely eliminate nicotine. It is the psychological addiction that is tough to treat and to overcome. This is why the chewing gum and skin patches have only about a 25%-35% success rate. That's right, 65%-75% of the people who start one of these programs eventually return to cigarettes.

Many people think smoking or chewing tobacco is a habit. It is not. A habit, as defined in Webster's dictionary, is an addiction, but that is next to last in the list of definitions of "habit." The first definition is "a type of dress clothing". The second definition is "a usual manner of behavior." Habits can be developed and broken. If one does not repeat the habit daily, it will usually be dropped without a craving to repeat it.

An addiction however, is a compulsive need to repetitively use or consume a substance. While generally thought of as a physical need, the psychological need is paramount and much more powerful, making it hard to conquer.

As mentioned earlier, finding relief from pain, as engaging in a pleasurable physical and/or emotional experience, is preferable to continued pain.

Most smokers have a psychological reversal regarding quitting smoking. They say that they want to stop, but subconsciously they do not want to stop. Others **want** to stop but **will not**. This is a deeper degree of psychological reversal, characterized by the smoker's fear that he/she will no longer have an easily accessible tranquilizer that needs no prescription.

I have had many patients say, "I want to stop, but if I do, I know that I will become very irritable and be obnoxious to my spouse, friends, children, co-workers, etc., so I can't do it. I have tried many times, but everyone says I turn into such a "bear" that they would rather have me keep smoking."

The Acu-POWER treatment actually balances the energies in the body so the individual can cope with his/her frustrations, anxieties, etc., so they will not turn into "bears". There is minimal, if any, irritability experienced.

Occasionally, I have found people who fear not smoking because they have depended on this tranquilizer for so long as a crutch. It is incomprehensible to these people that they could ever be without a cigarette. The fear so overwhelms them that they say, "I really want to stop smoking, but not now -- I have a lot of stressful things coming up and I just can't stop now. After all, stopping smoking is very stressful. I know because my friend (brother, sister, mother, father, son, daughter, cousin, boss) tried to stop and they were an emotional mess! I know I should stop, and I will someday -- just not now. I've got to want to stop before I try, isn't that right?"

The excuses can go on and on, but the reason for them is the fear that without cigarettes, they will not be able to function. If this is the case, the fear of not smoking must be treated first using the basic treatment in Chapter 10, which is the basis of the addiction treatment. Once this fear is overcome, if present at all, you are ready to proceed to treating the tobacco addiction.

To save time, the person should first be tested for psychological reversals. I say reversals because there can be several. Have the person say, "I want to stop smoking." If reversed, there will be weakness in the testing arm. It should be treated by having the person say, "I deeply accept myself even though I am a smoker." while tapping on the psychological reversal point (See Figures 12a&b). If the person stayed strong on "I want..." now have him/her say, "I will stop smoking." If the test arm weakens on this statement, the correct affirmation is, "I deeply accept myself even if I NEVER stop smoking," while tapping on the psychological reversal point (See Figures 12a&b).

Occasionally, some individuals are so literal in their interpretation that while they will stay strong on "I will stop smoking," will weaken on the statement, "I will stop smoking **today**."! If he/she weakens on this statement, the affirmation is, "I deeply accept myself even if I don't stop smoking today."

If the person stays strong on "I will..." have him/her say, "I deserve to stop smoking." If this weakens the test arm have him/her repeat the deserving affirmation in Chapter 11.

If the person stays strong on "I deserve..." Have him/her say, "Stopping smoking will be good for me." If this weakens the test arm the affirmation is, "I deeply accept myself even though I don't think stopping smoking will be good for me."

After all these possible psychological reversals are tested for and corrected, it is time to quantify the person's urge for the cigarette or chewing tobacco.

Have him/her quantify the urge or desire on a scale of 1-10, with "10" being the highest urge; that is, the cigarette must be smoked or the tobacco must be chewed. "1" would mean there is absolutely no urge or desire and if offered a cigarette he/she would not accept. If the urge starts out as only a "6", for instance, encourage the person to think about it and bring the urge or desire up as high as possible. Have the person continue to think of how good a cigarette would be and test the strong arm. It will be weak. Have the person place the fingers of the opposite hand on test point one, just above the navel. In most cases, the arm will now be strong while he/she is thinking of the cigarette. If not, proceed through the other eleven test points to find the one that will abolish the weakness. In most cases it will be test point one; if not, have the person tap on the respective treatment points of the test point that abolished the weakness (See Figures 8 a&b) while thinking of how GOOD the cigarette or chew would be. Keep reminding him/her to continue to concentrate on how good it would be, how relaxing it would be, how good it would taste, etc., while he/she is tapping.

After ten to fifteen seconds of tapping, ask where the urge is -- has it increased or decreased? In most cases, it will have decreased by least two points. In some cases, particularly when the original urge was "7" or below, the urge may have increased because the person was not really concentrating enough on the urge or desire at first. In this case continued tapping on the treatment point will lower it. If not, the person is psychologically reversed and must be treated. It is possible the person is not psychologically reversed at first, but once into the treatment suddenly became aware the treatment might work and really does not want to give up the crutch!

Have the person continue to tap the treatment points, but if progress stops and there is not a mini-reversal, it is now time to do the Brain Balance treatment (as described in Chapter 10) while thinking of having a cigarette or chew.

Continue the treatment until the person says he/she is at a "1", then have him/her say, "I am totally and completely free of all desire for a cigarette." The test arm should stay strong. If not, the person has not completely released all the anxiety causing the urge or desire for the cigarette. Continue treatment until this occurs. It usually will only take a minute to complete. If the urge does not go all the way down to a one, check for mini-reversal and/or to find if the treatment points have changed.

In more difficult cases, be sure to check for negative life beliefs (See Chapter 11), unresolved issues (See Chapter 12), and Post Traumatic Stress Syndromes (See Chapter 19), which may be at the core of the urge to smoke.

If you or the person you are treating are attending private counseling sessions, or group therapy such as Nicotinics Anonymous, Acu-POWER treatment will be a good adjunct.

Chapter 17

Alcohol Addiction

Alcoholism is probably the most denied addiction there is. Most individuals who are addicted to alcohol certainly deny it to themselves, and tell their loved ones or friends they are only social drinkers and can stop at anytime. They further delude themselves by rationalizing that almost 'everybody' has a drink at some time, that he/she likes the taste and enjoys the relaxation it gives after work. "Besides", they tell themselves, "I've earned it, haven't I?." "I can afford it." "I enjoy it." "It relaxes me." The list goes on and on.

There are many excuses for having a drink: It's 'attitude adjustment time'. It's 'happy hour'. I had a hard day at the office, factory, store, etc. My wife/husband doesn't understand me. I just broke up with my girlfriend/boyfriend. I can't forget the war and all the things I have seen and experienced. I need a drink to face this situation.

Recently, Mort Walker, creator of the Bettle Bailey comic strip, had General Halftrack at the bar in the officers' club saying to another officer, "Every morning I resolve to stop drinking, but then something stressful always happens to drive me to it." The other officer asks, "What happened today?" In the next panel it shows the General drinking his drink while saying, "We ran out of paper clips!"

As you can see, anxiety, no matter how trivial, can and is used for an excuse to drink. But more basically, any real or imagined anxieties or fears are the underlying cause of the desire for relief of the alcoholic's pain.

John Pursch, M.D., psychiatrist, states in his book Dear Doc... that most doctors who treat alcoholics have the 4-2-1-syndrome. They have studied four years in medical school, in which they have taken two hours of alcohol abuse study and expect to help or cure individuals of the number one addiction problem in the U.S.! He points out the absurdity of substituting one pill four times a day for one drink four times a day. The drugs which are prescribed -- Valium to "validate", Librium to "liberate", Elavil to "elevate" -- are all addicting in and of themselves. While seeming to change the individual, they only change the drug (alcohol) to a pill form.

Pursch also states that the saying, "relief is just a swallow away" is unfortunately believed by both doctor and patient. Continuing, he states that "most doctors give drugs to get rid of his own frustrations and you." He feels that the best way to treat the alcoholic is through counseling which is designed to help the addict cope with his/her problems, and with the help of AA. He further recommends that if drugs are prescribed that it be a minimum amount, under careful supervision and on a temporary basis.

Goodwin, in his book Is Alcohol Hereditary? (Ballantine) describes two types of alcoholics -- Type 1: non-familial (acquired), usually beginning in the mid-twenties; and Type 2: familial (hereditary), usually beginning in adolescence or early twenties. Type 2 is more severe.

There is disagreement among researchers regarding the heredity factor but the results of several studies, namely the Danish, Swedish and Iowa studies came to the conclusion that children - more specifically, sons of alcoholics - became alcoholics four to five times more frequently than children of non-alcoholics, even when brought up by non-relatives (Goodwin). In all of these studies the subjects studied were adopted in infancy and never knew their biological alcoholic parents.

Additionally, Henri Begleiter, M.D. and associates of the Downstate Medical Center of the University of New York in Brooklyn studied known alcoholics and found that there was a 300 millisecond delay in the P-300 wave of the brain. He wondered if sons of alcoholics might inherit the same deficiency. He then examined two hundred sons of alcoholics, ranging in age from six to late adolescence. The group was composed of males who had never consumed alcohol. There was a control group of two hundred males from non-alcoholic families who also had not yet had alcohol. Each subject was fitted with sensory apparatus to measure the amplitude of the P-300 wave. The sons of the alcoholics had a 300 millisecond diminished amplitude response of the P-300 wave to a click of light, as compared the sons of the non-alcoholics. The conclusion was that the brains of the sons of the alcoholics, like known alcoholics, did not organize a response to the stimuli (light click) as well as the brains of the control subjects (Goodwin). While this does not positively prove that a diminishment of the P-300 wave in a individual will cause them to be an alcoholic, it suggests a strong relationship. There have been at least six additional studies with the same outcome.

This is particularly important due to the nature of addicts, particularly those who use alcohol and or drugs. There is an argument among the various experts as to the question of 'nature' or 'nurture'. Those that say it is an inborn physiological defect are right and those who say that it is a matter of how one was brought up, whether they learned wrong from right, whether they had a tough environment, etc. are also right. Each viewpoint has arguments pointing toward a conclusion.

The poorly designed Sobel experiment attempted to show that alcoholics could be "cured" so that they could become rational social drinkers, that alcoholism was caused from some outside force or influence and was not genetic or inherited. The Sobel experiment was a very small study of only twenty people who were alcoholics. It was hypothesized that addiction was a behavioral problem and that once the behavior had been changed, the alcoholic could be "cured" so they could then be responsible social drinkers, that is, be able to drink with control on a social basis. At first it looked like the researchers had proven their point -- that an alcoholic could be cured by a behavior modification program.

Shortly after the completion of the treatment program which was sponsored by a major distillery and a $500,000. government grant, all the individuals were personally contacted by phone or mail. Their responses indicated all had been "cured."

Later, another group of researchers followed up by personally contacting the families and friends of the subjects in the experiment -- they found some strikingly different results. The follow-up researchers discovered that of the group of twenty, fourteen were dead, five were practicing alcoholics and one had remained sober through joining AA.

The Rand Report, a study on whether alcoholics could resume responsible drinking, showed conclusively that when alcoholics drink again they tend to get drunk again and end up worse than before (Pursch).

In 1978 while doing brain cancer research, a researcher in Houston, Texas discovered a natural substance called tetrahydroisoquinalones (THIQS). He had discovered this substance - which is known to be the product of cellular breakdown in heroin addicts - while dissecting the bodies of unclaimed bodies in the morgue. These research subjects were usually known alcoholics. Once THIQS are manufactured by the brain tissue, the substance almost never leaves. It remains for life. This substance is know to cause physical addiction.

There are a number of reasons why a person is, or becomes predisposed to becoming, addicted to alcohol. Without getting into a detailed chemical discussion, I will briefly review the process used to breakdown alcohol so that it can be processed through the body. First the alcohol is changed to acid aldehyde, an irritant, which causes a person to get "high" on alcohol. Since acid aldehyde is an irritant, the body then breaks it down to carbon dioxide (which is eliminated through the lungs), water, (which is eliminated by the kidneys) and acetic acid (which is used in the acetic acid cycle). Part of the acid aldehyde combines with dopamine in the brain and forms

THIQ. Since the THIQ is known to create addictive tendencies and is accumulative, that is, never leaves the body, the more one consumes alcohol the more possibility there is to become an alcoholic.

There is another factor working in the body of an alcoholic. As a child, did you ever wonder how your mother knew you were in the cookie jar even when you had very carefully rearranged the cookies so she wouldn't notice any were missing? Mom knew you had taken the cookies, by the crumbs that were left behind in the jar.

Metabolites, the by-products of cell function, leave debris (crumbs) called free radicals. These attach to the fat cells until the individual is under STRESS -- then they are released into the blood stream. Because they have enough of the original substance from which they were formed, they have a molecular identity and are recognized as the drug of preference (alcohol or other drugs) at the neurotransmitter site. This causes a physiological urge that seems to come out of nowhere.

It was found that the induction of THIQ (which acts like the metabolites) into the bodies of non-alcoholic mice - mice that were bred not to drink alcohol - turned into uncontrollable alcoholics if as little as three percent alcohol was added to their water!

It is important to understand that while emotional pain is the underlying cause for a person to seek relief in alcohol, some individuals have an additional burden of a genetic factor. *In either case the trigger is the emotional pain.* For those who have the predisposing genetic factor, treatment will be usually more difficult and lengthy.

Until now, the most dependable voluntary program was the twelve step Alcoholics Anonymous program, which has helped millions of people to abstain from alcohol. It is still very good but the addition of the Acu-POWER procedures will help make the process faster and more effective.

As with all the Acu-POWER procedures, test for neurological disorganization as described in Chapter 9 before proceeding.

As in the AA program, the first thing a person must do is acknowledge that he/she has a problem, that he/she is an alcoholic. I have never encountered an alcoholic who has not been psychologically reversed to some degree. The next thing to do is to test for the various degrees of psychological reversal (See Chapter 9) by having the person say the following statements:

1. I want to stop drinking alcohol.
2. I will stop drinking alcohol.
3. My stopping drinking alcohol will be good for me.
4. Stopping my drinking alcohol will be good for others.
5. I deserve to stop drinking alcohol.
6. It is possible for me to stop drinking alcohol.

In most cases one or more of the statements will make an indicator muscle weak when tested. If there is a weakness to one or more of these statements, this psychological reversal must be treated first. If not, treatment is ready to begin.

The following affirmations will be most effective for the respective statements that tested weak:

1. I Deeply accept myself even though I drink alcohol.
2. I deeply accept myself even if I never stop drinking alcohol.
3. I deeply accept myself even though I drink alcohol and I don't think it will be good for me to stop drinking.
4. I deeply accept myself even though I drink alcohol and I don't think it will be good for others if I stop drinking.
5. I deeply accept myself even though I drink alcohol and don't think I deserve to be sober.
6. I deeply accept myself even though I drink alcohol and don't think it is possible to stop drinking.

You may think of some other appropriate affirmations - if you do, try them.

Have the person say the affirmation three times, with meaning, whether he/she believes it or not, while tapping on the psychological reversal point (See Figures 12 a&b). Retest on the same statement and the indicator muscle should now test strong. If not, repeat the psychological reversal procedure and test again.

Now the person is ready to begin the actual treatment. Have him/her think of their favorite drink and rate their desire to have that drink on a scale of '1' to '10', '10' being the highest desire and '1' no desire at all. Have the person think of their favorite drink again and test an indicator muscle (See Figures 6 a&b). It will be weak. Start with therapy localizing test point one (See Figure 8a), and if that strengthens the weak indicator muscle, proceed with the treatment; if not, continue to therapy localize the test points until one is found that strengthens the indicator muscle. Have him/her tap on the corresponding treatment points (See Figure 8b) while thinking of how good it would be to have a drink, how relaxing it would be, how good it would taste, etc. Ask the person to quantify the desire again and note the change. It will usually go down one or two points in about fifteen seconds. Occasionally, if it began at a six or seven, for instance, after being reminded to think of how good it would be, the desire might go up at first, but will come down after further treatment. As in the addiction for food or tobacco, continue with all the procedures until the desire is at a '1', and the indicator muscle remains strong while he/she states, "I have completely and totally released (lost) all my desire for alcohol. You may, in some cases, have to specifically name each type of drink the person likes, such as Scotch, Martini, bourbon, rye, Canadian, wine, beer, etc. Test the indicator muscle, and if the statement is actually true, the muscle will be strong. If there is weakness, there is still a small desire for the alcohol and you must test for a mini-reversal, a change in treatment points, or a need to do the Brain Balance procedure. Usually the desire is somewhere between a one and a two, so start testing by asking the person to say, "My desire for_____ is a one and three-fourths." If the indicator muscle is strong, that is where he/she is and the mini-reversal is treated. If the indicator muscle was not strong when saying it was at one and three fourths, progress downward by increments of one fourth until you get a strong response and then treat for the mini-reversal. See Chapter 9.

At this point you might find that the person will have a number of mini-reversals, because it may be very difficult for them to give up all of their "crutch" and start taking total responsibility of their lives.

Recently, I read a letter to Ann Landers from Lyle Prouse, a former captain of Northwest Airlines who, with his crew, was convicted of flying while alcohol-impaired. The case made international headlines because the safety of the passengers and the people on the ground were in peril, had the airliner crashed. Fortunately, there was no crash, but the possibility was there. In his letter, Prouse described his efforts to lead a group of fellow prison inmates in a weekly program to help overcome their drug and alcohol problems. I found the most significant statement he made in the letter to be, "....all alcoholics and addicts are responsible for their actions."

This means that conquering the addiction - complete abstinence to alcohol or any other substance - regardless of whether the addiction is genetic, hereditary or the result of environmental, social, behavioral, emotional or psychological stresses, is the sole responsibility of the individual.

There is much help and assistance for the individual to seek and receive, but the individual is ultimately responsible for taking the action to help him/her self. At any point, from the beginning all the way through the treatment, as I mentioned before, the fear of not having a "crutch" of alcohol must be tested for and treated. Have the person make the statement, "I have a fear of losing my crutch of alcohol" and test a strong muscle. If it stays strong, the statement is true. Have the person think of their fear of not having alcohol to fall back on and test again. This time the muscle will weaken. Check for psychological reversal regarding the fear and treat if necessary. Find the test point that abolishes the weakness while the person is thinking of this fear and then treat the respective points for that fear.

In some rare cases, the treatment described may be all that is needed to completely cure them and they will never have another urge to drink. This is ideal but not common. Every time the individual has the urge to have a drink there will be accompanying anxiety that is causing pain or discomfort. The person remembers that alcohol reduced or stopped the pain in the past, and he/she will be tempted to use it again. In any of these cases, he/she should be instructed to immediately treat themselves for psychological reversal by saying, "I deeply accept myself even though I have a strong urge for_____", while tapping on the psychological reversal point (See Figures 12 a&b). It is then time to start tapping treatment point "1," just under the eyes (See Figure 8b), while thinking of how much he/she wants the drink. If the urge has not been reduced at all in fifteen to thirty seconds, the person must be tested for the specific point to be treated.

Many people who are addicted to alcohol have one or more negative life beliefs, unresolved issues, post traumatic syndromes, love pain, or rejection which need to be tested for and treated. Refer to the chapters that cover those subjects, and you will find that this may be the rest of the answer.

One of the women of a alcohol recovery group I mentioned in Chapter 11 who didn't feel that she deserved happiness - later was found to have two negative life beliefs - that she was a victim and that she was not a worthy person. She seemed to always put herself in a position of servitude whether it be to her alcoholic husband or anyone else. For example, a friend allowed her to rent an apartment from him without making the usual deposit of $200.00 and the last month's rent. Very soon after moving in, the landlord, a 72 year old man began to ask for help with his house work, cooking, shopping, getting things for him around the house, running errands, and taking him to his children's homes one hundred miles away. What started as a few hours a day soon became a fourteen to sixteen hour a day job for which she was not being paid. She discovered that if she did not answer her door at 5:30 AM when he was knocking, he would come to her bedroom window and call for her to get up and fix his breakfast!

She related to the group that she was getting very angry and resentful but didn't know how to stop him from intruding in her life without hurting his feelings. She felt that she still owed him because he did not charge her a deposit and the last months rent. The group pointed out that even at minimum wage of $4.25 an hour, she had given him about $3,100 in services in return for his waiving the $200 deposit and the last month's rent (which was about $300). This incident reenforced the fact that she believed she was a victim, and not a worthy person. In her effort to prove to him she was a worthy person she was giving far beyond her need and she was resenting it (being a victim).

In any type of addiction, one of the most precipitating feelings that will trigger the use of the addictive substance is resentment. She was treated for the negative life beliefs that she was unworthy and a victim, and this put her in control so that she could lay down boundaries. She finally communicated with this man and let him know she would be happy to help him on her terms, but she was not his indentured servant.

Alcohol, unlike food, is not necessary for life. Like to-bacco, it can be eliminated from use, "cold turkey". If the individual has consumed alcohol heavily for a long period of time, there usually will be a need for supervised detoxification. High dosages of vitamin C, B complex and water are very essential during this period. In some severe cases, the person may have to be hospitalized during the "drying-out" process -- or at least confined to their homes.

There are usually several layers of emotions that may be treated before you uncover the real problem; this takes time. As with any addiction, if you or whomever you are presently working with on this problem are in regular treatment, do not abandon it but use this Acu-POWER procedure to speed the recovery.

During and after the treatment for all the fears, phobias, anxieties, negative life beliefs, issues and post traumatic syndromes, be sure that the individual is on an optimal diet: fresh fruits and vegetables, whole grains, foods rich in tryptophane such as bananas and milk, some (but not too much) meat, poultry or fish, and avoidance of sugar and sugar containing products as well as processed foods (these foods will produce free radicals).

Also, since vitamin C is an excellent detoxifier, it is important that supplemental C is taken. Start with 1000 milligrams a day and gradually build up to 3,000 milligrams or more, if possible. If diarrhea occurs, cut back the dosage until the diarrhea stops, then gradually increase the dosage. After detoxifying, it is important that the dosage of vitamin C be brought down gradually to a maintenance dose. Check with your doctor. As mentioned previously, supplementation with the B complex is also necessary.

To Summarize, there are four basic causes of alcoholism:

1. Bio-genetic -- which is hereditary. It includes THIQ, which can come from the drinking of alcohol or be passed on in the genes and control our compulsions, sensitivities and mood swings, and P-300 deficit in the brain, which effects the interpretation of stimuli.

2. Psychological, which comes from our base patterning, our life beliefs. (These are the things from which everything else is built).

3. Emotional, based on psychological results of how we deal with life's experiences - good or bad -on a basis of our feelings.

4. Sociological (standards by which we conduct life), which comes from the attitudes, behaviors, from parents, peers, church, society, work, friends, authoritative individuals.

As you can see, three of the basic causes involve feelings and beliefs. These are the factors that can be treated with the Acu-POWER procedures.

Alcoholism is like diabetes in a way. If a person is diabetic, one way to control the symptoms of sugar abuse is by not eating sugar. The person still has diabetes but is non-symtomatic. The only way an alcoholic can control the symptoms of alcohol abuse by not drinking alcohol - complete abstinence.

Stress, anxiety, fear and all the other emotional conflicts are the precursors of the use and abuse of alcohol, along with the built-in factors of genetic origin. It is evident that if there is a faster way of reducing or abolishing the stress-factor of alcoholism, programs such as the twelve step AA program or treatment by individual professionals or alcohol treatment centers, would be greatly enhanced by its use. Acu-POWER is a fast and effective tool to deal with these problems, and should be used to compliment and enhance any alcohol abuse treatment program.

Chapter 18

Drug Addiction

Drug addiction, like any other addiction, is generally the result of unresolved anxieties, fear, negative life beliefs, post traumatic stress syndrome, or anything else an individual cannot cope with -- including physical pain.

Unfortunately, from the time we are old enough to understand, we are bombarded with advertisements telling us, "Don't cope, take dope!" "Relief is just a swallow away." The medical profession also sends us similar messages -- Can't sleep? Take a downer. Can't stay awake? Take an upper. Anxious? Take a tranquilizer. In pain? Take a pain reliever. Sidney Harris, a nationally syndicated columnist, once confirmed this attitude in a column he titled "America's number one 'drug pusher'". In it, he named medical doctors as America's number one drug pushers. Only those involved in the alternative health movement teach that there are other ways to cope with physical pain and the trials and tribulations of life.

Peer pressure usually causes young people to start taking drugs, because it seems exciting. Peers say, "Come on, everybody's doing it -- let's get high, it feels so good!" Or, they suggest that problems will disappear simply by taking a few appropriate pills.

From there on, behavioral changes will be obvious - not to the user, but to friends and family. Emotional isolation is soon followed by impaired reasoning and movement. Dependency builds with increasing frequency and strength of dosage.

When approached regarding the drug use, users will deny and cover up their problem. But even more destructive is self denial. As time goes on, users begin to fear there is no life without drugs.

Drug addiction crosses all social, economic, professional and political boundaries. James Dewitt, M.D., author of the book Addict, A Doctor's Odyssey, started taking pain killers to ease the back and leg pain he suffered as a result of a disc problem. Soon, he became both physiologically and psychologically addicted to the drugs. When they began to lose effectiveness, he turned to alcohol. In the end he lost his wife, his home, his practice and his medical license. He had gone as low as forging prescriptions and stealing drugs. Finally, he wound up commuting between jail and the hospital. Having hit rock bottom, he met a woman who was also an alcoholic. They conquered their addictions together.

The road to recovery was long and treacherous, but he survived, and in the end regained his sobriety and his medical license. He has since dedicated his life to helping other addicts. Dr. Dewitt's struggle took place in the '50s - long before Acu-POWER was developed.

Treating drug addiction is similar to treating food, tobacco and alcohol addictions. But instead of thinking of those substances, you think of the drug that you are using and how good you feel when you are using it, as was explained with the other addictive substances.

Drug addicts usually experience a great physical as well as psychological addiction; it may not be possible to quit 'cold turkey'. Consult a physician. Complete supervision is definitely necessary when someone quits using an addictive substance cold turkey.

There are usually several layers of emotions that must be treated before reaching the addict's underlying problem -- this takes time. As with any addiction, if you or someone you are presently working with has a drug problem and is being treated in a program, do not abandon it, but use Acu-POWER in conjunction with it to speed recovery.

Chapter 19

Post Traumatic Stress Syndrome

"If you are distressed by anything external,
the pain is not due to the thing itself but to
your own estimate of it; and this you have
the power to revoke at any moment."

Marcus Aurelius

All the feelings felt in the aftermath of accidents, war, death, sexual abuse, rape, child abuse, grief and love pain can be summed up in the frustrating, self pitying thought of "If only."

If only I had not been there. If only I had resisted more. If only I had taken care of my equipment better. If only I had paid more attention to him/her. If only I had said... These are but a variation of "why did it happen to me?"

There can be a variety of emotions that are felt: self pity, anger, resentment, desire for revenge, confusion, grief, fear, dread, bitterness, unworthiness, victimized, used, damaged - the list goes on and on.

There are many people who never seem to be able to rise above these negative emotions and go on with their lives. They wallow in circumstances rather than taking charge of their lives. Many well-meaning friends, relatives and counselors tell them to "get hold of yourself", "snap out of it" or the more benevolent, "have faith, this too shall pass". Sometimes this works, but in many cases it doesn't.

When someone has experienced a physical and or emotional trauma, he/she either accepts the situation and grows from it, or is crushed by it, leaving an unbalanced energy which never resolves the issue. The Greek philosopher, Epictetus said, "People do not get disturbed by the things that happen to them, but by their view of those things." Shakespeare put it in slightly different words, "It is our opinion of things which distress us, not the things themselves."

In Bill Moyers book, Healing and The Mind, Margaret Remeny states, "The mind and the body are two manifestations of the same process. Even to say they are "interconnected" is improper, because they are two parts of one whole." Because of this, the mind/body will keep issues on or near the surface where it influences every decision or bury them in the subconscious where it may fester for years only to attempt to surface in some other way, sometimes physical and sometimes emotional. High blood pressure, asthma, skin conditions, digestive disorders, constipation, diarrhea, heart disease, arthritis, visual problems and blindness are a few examples of the physical symptoms.

For example, Paul Harvey, on his popular radio show, "The Rest of The Story," told of a young black boy who got distracted for a few minutes when he was supposed to be watching his younger brother, who was playing in a tub of water. In those few minutes, the younger brother slipped and drowned. The older brother was so distraught by the event (not *watching* his brother), that within a very short time he became totally blind. The older brother's name is Ray Charles.

Emotionally, symptoms can come in the form of anxiety attacks, phobias, or the inability to succeed. It can also prevent one from having meaningful relationships in anything from friendship to marriage. It can lead to addictions of all kinds as you have read in previous chapters.

As with any of the previous treatment procedures, the first thing to do is to have the person rate their degree of pain, anxiety, grief, fear or whatever the negative emotion is on a scale of '1' to '10' regarding the incident, '10' being the highest and '1' being the lowest (none at all, totally relaxed).

To save time, test for neurological disorganization and psychological reversal to be sure that he/she wants to deal with the problem (See Chapter 9); then you are ready to begin. Most instances of post traumatic stress syndrome are composed of more than one event or issue. To begin, have the person start with what he/she feels is most disturbing. As soon as the event or issue is rated on a scale of '1' to '10', have the person think of the event or issue and test a strong indicator muscle (See Figures 6 a&b). It should become weak. If it doesn't, recheck for neurological disorganization and treat to correct it (See Chapter 9). Now with the indicator muscle becoming weak while thinking of the event or issue, have him/her touch test point one (See Figure 8a) with the opposite hand. If the indicator muscle strengthens, the person proceeds with tapping the treatment points just under the eyes (See Figure 8b). If not, proceed with touching the various test points until one is found that strengthens the indicator muscle; have the patient tap the corresponding treatment points.

After about fifteen seconds of tapping, ask the person to reevaluate the degree of pain, anxiety, or fear and continue treatment until there is no more pain, anxiety or fear. If progress stops, check for a mini-reversal and correct if necessary. Or, begin the brain balance procedure (See Figure 11). If there is still no progress, the person has moved to a different part of the event or issue and must be re-tested for new treatment points. You will find the original test point will no longer strengthen the indicator muscle (while thinking of the problem). Proceed testing until one is found that will. Have the person tap the new pair of treatment points and proceed as before.

There may be a multifaceted problem in any post traumatic stress syndrome, involving massive psychological reversal, or one or more negative life beliefs and several life issues. All of these must be tested and treated. See the corresponding chapters for details of testing and treatment. Often, the various flower remedies will be very helpful in keeping the problem from returning (See Chapter 14).

As you can see, the same basic procedures are used over and over. The only thing that changes is what the person is thinking about while he/she is tapping. If you have questions regarding the procedure, refer to the corresponding chapters for the precise treatment procedures.

ACCIDENTS

In the area of accidents, as in any beginning of treatment, the person should be asked if he/she wants to get over the emotional pain. After receiving permission and checking for the possibility of psychological reversal, ask him/her to quantify the degree of emotional pain on a scale of one to ten. Next, have him/her think of the actual event and test a strong indicator muscle -- it should become weak. Ask him/her to put the opposite hand on test point '1' (see Figure 8a) while thinking of the accident, and test. If the arm becomes strong, have him/her tap the treatment points under the eyes (See Figure 8b). If not, proceed to the other test points until one restores strength to the indicator muscle and have him/her tap the appropriate treatment points.

In most cases, this and the regular treatment procedure will correct the problem. However, in some cases you will have to ask the person to think of various aspects of the accident. For example, what was the person doing at the time? Did he/she see the accident coming? Ask about the impact, the immediate aftermath, who else was with them, the ride to the hospital or doctors office, the physical treatment, the impact of what was said by the rescue workers, the emergency room staff, the doctors, anything and everything that might have influenced the person. You will, by the use of muscle testing, be able to test any aspect of the accident to find out if it is still having an influence and know when it has been cleared. In any type of physical accident there is usually some physical trauma. Some is visible from the outside or on x-ray, C.A.T. scans or on MRI's. Some distortions of the cranium, however, can only be discovered by doctors trained in applied kinesiology, occipital sacral technique or osteopathic craniology. If these physical distortions of the skull are present, they may prevent or interfere with the Acu-POWER treatment. If there is any history of physical trauma and the person is not responding to Acu-POWER procedures, referral to a chiropractic or osteopathic physician trained in the above procedures is necessary. I once tested a patient who was having anxiety attacks just thinking of taking a test which she had to pass to become a licensed insurance representative. I could not treat her successfully with Acu-POWER procedures until I treated the cranial distortion.

You can find out who is trained in applied kinesiology in your area by calling or writing to the International College of Applied Kinesiology, P.O. Box 905, Lawrence KS 66044-0905. Telephone (913) 542-1801.

WAR

War is a very complex series of events that may consist of both physical and emotional trauma. The term "post traumatic stress syndrome" was coined as a result of the physical and psychological effects of the Vietnam war. Actually, it is just a new name for an old problem. In World War II, it was called "combat fatigue" and in World War I, it was called "shell shock."

The American Psychiatric Association, in its <u>Diagnostic and Statistical Manual (DSM) III</u>, published in 1980, defines post traumatic stress syndrome as "the development of characteristic symptoms following a psychologically traumatic event that is 'generally outside of human experience'." The editors of DSM III go on to define the acute phase of the disorder, "where the onset of the symptoms occurs within 6 months of the trauma and last less than 6 months, and the chronic or delayed phase, where symptoms either last 6 months or more, or manifest themselves at least 6 months after the trauma." <u>(The Vietnam Veteran Redefined, Fact & Fiction</u>, edited by Ghislaine

Boulanger & Charles Kadushin, Lawrence Erlbaum Associates, Publishers 1986 Hillsdale, N.J.)

Now that we have post traumatic stress syndrome "officially" defined, we can get on to the work at hand: fixing the problem!

Because of the diversity of experiences both male and female have, treating post traumatic stress syndrome of war is multifaceted. Each event must be dealt with individually and as completely as possible. Therefore, the person beginning treatment should be advised that the treatment process will probably be lengthy in relation to the speed of treating a single issue. In comparison to the length of orthodox treatment procedures, however, it is very short.

As a result of the emotional trauma, anxiety and depression, many individuals have resorted to compulsive behavior and or addictive personalities as their tranquilizers. Each of these must be treated individually.

After completing the initial procedures, it is best to let the person choose where to begin. Some want to take the least painful path; others want to jump right into the heart of the problem. Let the person decide.

In treating any kind of post traumatic stress syndrome, it is necessary to check for psychological reversal first (See Chapter 9.). Test by asking the patient to state: "I want to get over this, I will get over this, I will allow myself to get over this, I deserve to get over this, getting over this will be good for me, getting over this will be good for others, it is possible for me to get over this." The indicator muscle remaining strong indicates a true statement (See Figure 6b). If it weakens (See Figure 6c), proceed with treating and correcting the psychological reversal.

In any kind of a war trauma or accident where someone else was badly injured or died, the person may believe that he/she does not deserve to be alive, or should have died instead of, or as well as the other person. This also applies to injury to someone else whether or not the person being treated was injured, but particularly if the person was not injured. How many times have you heard someone say, "If anyone should have died, it should have been me!", or "I don't deserve to be alive." If a person makes a statement like this, test to find if he/she really believes this. If so (the indicator muscle will remain strong), have him/her reverse the statement. For example, "I deserve to be alive." The indicator muscle will now weaken. Find the test point that strengthens (See Figure 8a) and have him/her tap on the corresponding treatment points (See Figure 8b) while thinking of being alive, being spared, or uninjured. Proceed through the treatment procedure until he/she remains strong on the statement, "I deserve to be alive, uninjured, spared."

GUILT

Guilt, whether appropriate or not, must be tested for and treated if found. In post traumatic stress syndrome, guilt is a common emotion and issue. Even if it is applicable, it must be treated so that the person can accept forgiveness.

SEXUAL ABUSE

Sexual abuse can start at any age, and often continues for long periods of time. It happens within rich or poor families, rural and urban families. Probably one of the most notorious sexual abuse cases in recent history was that of a past Miss America and her sisters, who were sexually abused by their father, a wealthy and "respected man of the community" in Colorado. The emotional scars are far uglier than any physical ones.

Treating for sexual abuse, whether the victim is a child or now an adult, must be done with tact and gentleness. Permission from the person must always be requested and received before beginning. Often the person has no idea why he/she is in physical pain or emotional pain, and does not even suspect that this pain originates from sexual abuse. Sometimes, the victim is in denial and cannot even recall being sexually abused, because the incident(s) were so devastating they have completely blocked them out of their conscious mind. On the other hand, some people can vividly remember every heartbreaking detail.

I remember a 42 year old professional woman who was sexually abused as a child, and remembered the incidents very well. Earlier in her life she became alcoholic. When I met her, she had been sober for thirteen years thanks to the help of Alcoholics Anonymous. She had been married four times, but never had a good lasting relationship with a man. In addition, her professional practice was also suffering. She asked me to check her to see if the sexual abuse was interfering with her life. It was. We quickly found the test point that abolished the weakness. In *less than five minutes* she released all her negative emotions. The next day, she told me that for the first time in her adult life, she felt that she was grounded, that is, felt that she was standing on solid ground. She explained that at first it was like walking through mud, but later that day felt like she was standing and walking on solid ground.

Sexual abuse will cause many men and women to build a physical or emotional wall around themselves for protection so that it can never happen again. Often the result is carrying extra weight, from just a few pounds to being really obese. A very attractive female psychological counselor carries an extra fifteen to twenty pounds to "ward off" unwanted advances, even though she is happily married and intellectually knows her sexual abuse is the cause of her extra weight. Another person, on the other end of the scale carries about 200 extra pounds to protect her! Many of these victims shun close relationships, and if they find themselves getting too close or intimate, they will either subtly or grossly sabotage the relationship.

It is best, once the person knows you are going to be treating for the sexual abuse, to have him/her make the statement, "I'm ready to deal with this issue now." and test to see that the indicator muscle remains strong. If not, you might want to postpone treatment at that time, or ask the patient's permission to treat him/her for psychological reversal regarding the timing. After receiving permission, have the person say, "I deeply accept myself even though I do not want to deal with this problem now", while tapping on the psychological reversal point (See Figures 12 a&b). This, with the possible addition of giving him/her rescue remedy, will usually break through the fear of starting treatment.

In addition to treating the event itself, there is usually one or more negative life beliefs and or issues to be treated, which have been brought on by the abuse. These usually are that of being a victim, being used, being worthless, being bad, being guilty, being unlovable, etc. Refer to Chapter 11 and Chapter 12.

CHILD ABUSE

Child abuse, like sexual abuse, results in physical and emotional problems, and should be treated delicately. If the abused is a minor, it is necessary to have permission of a parent or guardian and, ideally, to have a non-involved adult nearby -- a family member, if possible -- so the child feels secure.

Treatment will follow the same or similar procedure as in sexual abuse.

RAPE

Rape victims, in many cases, have been made to feel that he/she, and particularly she, has brought it on herself by being too friendly, wearing "provocative" clothing, walking in a sensual way, and all the other accusations that are brought upon the victim, sometimes even by the police investigating the crime; and certainly by the defense attorney of the rapist, as the case goes to trial.

Rape victims usually carry a number of emotional issues and negative life beliefs after the event. Most common are anger, fear, resentment, guilt, being a victim, being used, being soiled and/or damaged and having no identity. There can be many others. See Chapter 11 for other negative life beliefs.

In the case of rape, as with sexual abuse, permission should be obtained before treating and the treatment should proceed as described in the sexual abuse section.

GRIEF

Grief from the loss (death) of a loved one, whether human or animal, can be devastating. Whether it happened recently or years ago makes no difference. Most psychologists and psychiatrists feel that in the event of a loss, whether it be of a loved one, friend, pet or inanimate things such as businesses or homes or other personal property, it takes a period of grieving to heal. I heartily agree, but only in that one must go through it. It is not necessary that it take weeks, months or years. By balancing energies, the grieving process can be shortened considerably. The grieving process is the act of accepting the loss both intellectually and emotionally. The length of time is indirectly proportionate to the degree of balance one has, to face and accept the loss. If one's energies are so out of balance (very little balance) that he/she cannot come to terms with the loss, then the time it takes to heal will be lengthy.

In treating grief, as with any other emotion, it is necessary to get permission from the person and find out if he/she is ready. In most cases, when the person is thinking of the grief and the strong indicator muscle becomes weak (See Figure 6c), having him/her touch one of the two LUNG test points (See Figure 8a), will usually strengthen the muscle, since this energy meridian is associated with grief. If neither does, proceed to the other energy test points until one is found to strengthen the indicator muscle. Proceed with the basic treatment in Chapter 10 until there is no more grief, that is, until the person has fully accepted the loss and can proceed with his/her life.

If the person does not get all the way down to a '1' on the scale, other facets of the grief involved, such as guilt, anger, resentment, etc., that need to be addressed and treated.

LOVE PAIN

Love pain can be, perhaps, the most intense and debilitating emotional pain one can suffer. Whether it is due to breaking up a marriage, an engagement, or a relationship or loving from afar, with the object of one's love not even aware of it, it is felt by almost everyone sometime in his/her life. It can be the pain of rejection, separation or not achieving the relationship one desires because of fear or shyness. Love pain can cause individuals to become 'stalkers' - to take the attitude that, "If I can't have her/him, then no one can." In such cases, the individual actually attempts or commits assault or murder. It can also result in a person being suicidal. To a lesser degree, but with just as much pain, some people "moon" over the loss, whether real or imagined. The term, "love sick" is very appropriate. As the song says, "Breaking Up Is Hard To Do."

Being rejected in love cuts to the very foundation of one's self worth, which can cause a person to wallow in self pity or become extremely belligerent or defensive. This is seen throughout the entire population regardless of gender, race or age. After being hurt, some people try to relieve the pain with food or tobacco or alcohol or drugs or all of the above.

Sometimes it is not a matter of being rejected, but having to leave a relationship because the other party is manipulating, using or abusing you, and to remain in such a relationship would be self-destructive. When a person is in this type of relationship, they often deny there is a problem. Such denial needs to be tested for and corrected first. It can be done by having the person say, "I am denying that _____ is manipulating, (using or abusing) me." Test a strong indicator muscle and if the statement is true the muscle will remain strong. You need to reverse the question to, "I am not denying that I am being manipulated (used or abused) by _____." If the statement is false the muscle will become weak. This indicates psychological reversal. Treat by having the person say, "I deeply accept myself even though I deny that _____ is manipulating (using or abusing) me," while tapping on the psychological reversal points (See Figures 12 a&b). After the psychological reversal has been cleared, have the person think of the manipulation, etc., then find the test point that abolishes the weakness and tap on the corresponding treatment points.

After this is done, have the person think of the individual involved and visualize walking away from this individual and leaving the relationship. This will usually make the indicator muscle weak. If so, find the test point that abolishes the weakness and have the person tap on the corresponding treatment points until the weakness is gone.

There may be a feeling of sadness or grief following this, and that needs to be treated. (Refer to the previous description of grief treatment in this chapter.) When the grief is gone, the person will have a feeling of relief and calm.

As with all the other types of post traumatic syndromes, once the energies are balanced, healing can take place and the individual can go on with his/her life.

As always, get permission to begin treatment. The best starting place is to have the person think of the individual involved and test a strong indicator muscle (See Figures 6 b&c). It will become weak. Find the test point (See Figure 8a) that abolishes the weakness and treat the corresponding treatment points (See Figure 8b). In many cases, that will be all that is necessary, but in others, there may be additional points to be treated because of other issues or events involved. You will find that many of these individuals will have several mini-reversals; it seems there is a universal but paradoxical self-abusing desire to be miserable and try to hold on to the fantasy that "all could be right again if I just show that I am really in love with this person." The futility of this state of mind is expressed very well in the song "Prisoner of Love" sung by Perry Como and the popular country western songs, "Help Me Make It Through The Night", and "For The Good Times".

The desire to be recognized, accepted and loved is so overwhelming that it keeps these people in a false state of hope. Balancing left and right brain is very important so the logic and imagination can communicate to accept the situation and get on with life.

In many cases, it will be helpful to test for the use of the various flower remedies (See Chapter 14).

Chapter 20

Sales Rejection and Burnout

"Nothing happens until someone sells
something."

That statement is so basic that it is known universally, and applies to all economies. It doesn't matter how good a "mouse trap" you invent, no one will beat a path to your door until someone sells your product or idea. We are **all** sales people one way or another.

Most people think of a sales person as someone who has a product to sell. However, a person does not have to have a product to sell. To introduce any kind of idea, one must "sell" it to another. Professionals are also sales persons whether they are a doctor, lawyer, CPA, etc. Each has to "sell" his or her recommendations to the patient or client.

The biggest fear any salesperson has is hearing the word "no", of being rejected by a prospect. Whether this rejection occurs in the initial stages of making a sale -- for example, while trying to make an appointment, or whether the product or service is rejected after making the presentation -- this rejection causes pain and can lead to fear of contacting the next prospect.

A good salesperson is able to recover, move on to the next prospect and try again. If rejection happens too many times, however, even the good salesperson begins to get discouraged, and doubt starts to creep into his/her mind. Fearing the next rejection, the doubtful salesperson becomes reluctant to call for another appointment or knock on another door. It's impossible to calculate the loss that has been suffered by individuals and companies because of this fear.

I doesn't matter whether the salesperson is a beginner or a veteran; for most, sooner or later, the fear of rejection will be so great that many will not even attempt to make a another call. Obviously, this is tantamount to accepting a rejection.

In a salesperson, it is especially important to test and treat for psychological reversal before starting treatment, because a reversal is almost always there (see Chapter 9). After multiple rejections, a "what's the use" attitude sets in and colors every effort.

Once the psychological reversal is corrected, have the person think about their fear of rejection and test for weakness of the indicator muscle (See Figures. 6 b&c). Have him/her quantify their fear on a scale of one to ten as described in Chapter 8, Fig 9. Next, find the test point that abolishes the weakness (See Figure 8a) and have the person tap on the corresponding treatment points (See Figure 8b).

In most cases the fear will diminish on down to a one. If not, check for mini-reversals. In some cases, there may be a change of issues, requiring a change of treatment points. Continue until all fear is gone and the person can make the statement, "My fear of sales rejection is totally and completely gone." In testing the strong indicator muscle, it should stay strong.

The next most common obstacle to success in sales or in business is a self-imposed limit as to one's earning power. Unfortunately, many people have subconscious limits on how much they can or deserves to earn. These are usually acquired sometime in life by having someone of authority (a parent, teacher, clergy, or employer) make a direct or indirect statement regarding the persons ability or what he/she deserves. If the mind accepts this statement, it will cause the person to be limited -- just as if there was a glass ceiling preventing the person from climbing any higher. For diagnosis and treatment procedures for this problem, see Chapter 11, Negative Life Beliefs. As you can see, after referring to the list of negative life beliefs, there can be one or many that will cause a person to limit his or her ability to sell.

Some individuals have very specific fears regarding selling. For instance, some are afraid to call on individuals who are smarter or richer than they are. Some are afraid of meeting new people (strangers). Remember as children we were told not to talk to strangers? Some are afraid of using the telephone. Whatever the fear, it must be acknowledged and treated.

With the use of Acu-POWER procedures, you or your sales organization can overcome any problem that is keeping you from achieving your goals.

Chapter 21

Sports Barriers

Almost all obstacles and barriers that beset the athlete are **mental**, not physical. Most athletes fail to attain their goals because of the mental picture they have of their ability. They have one or more negative life beliefs such as, "I'm incapable," "I don't deserve...," "I'm a failure." Being psychologically reversed on a particular goal will also prevent the individual from achieving it. Negative life beliefs are just a deeper level of psychological reversal.

Certainly physical training is essential, and the body must be physically fit, but the mind must also believe that it can win or achieve the goal. As mentioned in his book, Quantum Healing Deepak Chopra, M.D., writes about boundaries. He says that individuals create their own 'Maya' or illusion, which in Sanskrit means "that which is not." He continues, explaining that 'Maya' is the illusion of boundaries, the creation of a mind that has lost the cosmic perspective. These boundaries prevent athletes or anyone, from achieving their goal.

There are a number of programs on the market to assist both the amateur and professional athlete. The most advertised is probably CyberVision. It is a good program, but will not work if the individual is psychologically reversed!

In working with any athlete, however, the first area to investigate is neurological organization (See Chapter 9.) Neurological disorganization must be corrected to enable physical and emotional correction to take place.

Psychological reversal in its various degrees must be tested for and treated; the extension of psychological reversal - negative life beliefs - must also be investigated. Often, when these are corrected, athletes will soar to great heights. There may be, however, one or more specific fears that must be dealt with individually. Determine what the fears are and treat as simple phobias as outlined in Chapter 10.

It must be remembered that the better the athlete is and the closer he/she gets to a goal, the more likely psychological reversals will set in. At this point, the use of flower remedies is to be considered, particularly rescue remedy from the Bach remedies. It has also been found that MinTran from Standard Process Company and MinBall from Nutri-West are effective in preventing recurrences of psychological reversal (See Chapter 14).

Robert Blaich, D.C., now practicing in Denver, has treated many world class athletes - and particularly cyclists - for their physical and psychological problems. After Alexi Grewal won the one hundred mile bicycle race in the 1984 Olympics, Alexi was very appreciative of Dr. Blaich's treatment, which helped Grewal finally achieve his long sought after goal.

It is my belief that individual athletes, and sometimes whole teams, suffer from psychological reversal when they go into a "slump." Most eventually pull themselves out but wouldn't it be better if they could be treated and emerge from the slump much sooner?

There are many phobias most athletes would not regard as such because they are too "macho", too proud. For instance, in baseball, some players fear getting hit by a ball. Obviously, the fear inhibits them from hitting or catching as well as they would if they did not have that fear. In many sports there is the possibility of being injured. When treating an athlete with this fear, you must consider all the possibilities.

Sports that are individual in nature such as golf require clear mental images of what is intended. Many golfers have a fear of not hitting the ball squarely and therefore hooking or slicing, going out of bounds, driving into the water or other hazards. This fear can make for a bad day on the golf course. Generally all that is needed is to treat oneself for psychological reversal regarding the specific fear and then test to determine which treatment points should be tapped to erase the fear. To be as inconspicuous as possible while you are on the course, I suggest the use of the 'O' ring self test as described in Chapter 24.

All athletes should be under chiropractic care - particularly by an applied kinesiologist or a certified chiropractic sports physician - for their physical needs. This, in combination with Acu-POWER procedures, lead to a winning combination.

Chapter 22

Academic Barriers

Like sports, academic barriers can prevent a person from even learning a particular subject, let alone getting high grades.

There are many people who are brilliant in many areas, but just can't seem to understand or learn a particular subject. For instance, when I was in high school, I couldn't seem to understand or learn chemistry equations. Fortunately, I spontaneously overcame this problem when I entered college. I not only didn't have any trouble learning how to balance chemistry equations, but I was tutoring others in my class in that area. Not everyone is so lucky and there are millions of brilliant students who, for one reason or another, are psychologically reversed when it comes to a particular subject.

The learning disabled or dyslexic person many times has a psychological reversal because they have failed so many times. Correcting the psychological reversal will be at least a step in the right direction. Usually these individuals have one or more neurological disorganization problems. In simple cases, correcting this as described in Chapter 9 can make a great difference so the individual can then go on to learn.

I am reminded of a 34 year old woman who has excelled in business. She was named Retail Entrepreneur of the Year in the Southwest Region by Inc. and Ernst & Young and was awarded the prestigious Blue Chip Award from the United States Chamber of Commerce. Even though she has been very successful in business, she was dyslexic and could only read on a fourth grade level. She had neurological disorganization and was psychologically reversed on reading. After treatment, she is now able to receive special tutoring so she can improve her reading ability.

Once the psychological reversal has been treated, there are usually simple phobias that can be treated using the basic Acu-POWER treatment as outlined in Chapter 10.

In more complicated cases, these individuals should be referred to a chiropractic physician who is an applied kinesiologist and also qualified in Neural Organization Techniques. Names and addresses of such doctors who are located in the United States, Europe and Australia can be obtained by writing or calling the developer, Carl Ferreri, D.C., 3850 Flatlands Ave. Brooklyn, NY 11234, Telephone (718) 253-9702. This author is qualified in these techniques.

There are many students who have phobias about tests. They know the material, but if they have to take a written or oral test, they become fearful, in some cases to the point of panic. This prevents them from achieving the higher grade score on a test. I had a friend in college who was so fearful at test time, he would become physically ill and vomit in anticipation of the test.

To treat for the phobia of taking tests, follow the basic Acu-POWER treatment procedure in Chapter 10.

As you can see, the Acu-POWER procedures can be helpful in any type of academic problem.

Chapter 23

Compulsive Behavior and Obsessive Thoughts

There are literally millions of nail biters, and they can be found all over the world. There are also hair pickers, hand washers, door lock checkers, etc., who practice compulsive rituals over and over and over and over. Compulsive behavior seems to calm anxiety for a short time, and temporarily relieve fears, phobias, anxieties, or other forms of psychological or emotional pain. The compulsive hand washers, for instance, usually have a phobia about dirt or germs which compels them to wash their hands far more frequently than necessary. It is an obsession with them.

In my clinical experience, I have found that anytime a person with any type of compulsive behavior thinks of that behavior, a strong indicator muscle will weaken. This is because the mind automatically goes to the phobia or anxiety -- even if it is subconscious. Sometimes the person has no conscious idea of why he/she is drawn to the compulsive act.

It also follows that if that person thinks of the compulsive act and puts a hand on the test points one by one, that one of the twelve test points will abolish the weakness in the indicator muscle; tapping the corresponding treatment points will reduce the urge to perform the compulsive act. Like any of the phobias, addictions or other problems that have been discussed in this book, the treatment point may change during the treatment process and there may be mini-psychological reversals during the process, or there may be a need for some flower remedy.

To treat a person or yourself for compulsive behavior it is necessary to think of the urge to do whatever it is that is compulsive and quantify it on a scale of '1' to '10'. Test for psychological reversal before beginning treatment. Correct it if necessary (See Chapter 9). Use the basic treatment procedure in Chapter 10 for the correction.

Remember that some compulsive behaviors are multi-faceted and will take several sessions of treatment, sometimes even going into treatment for negative life beliefs and issues before being completely successful.

COMPULSIVE GAMBLING

A recent television show, "Investigative Report", covering gambling in the United States, discussed the pros and cons of legalized gambling. It was estimated that 3 to 5 percent of people who gambled became compulsive gamblers, that is, addicted to gambling. It was said that these peoples' addictions are similar to alcoholic and drug addictions, implying that the availability of legalized gambling would "cause" them to become addicted.

Perhaps the temptation would make the addiction come on faster. It is my opinion that these individuals are gamblers already, and do, in fact, gamble on many other things of life before being addicted to the legalized casino gambling.

A compulsive gambler usually will gamble until he/she has lost all they have -- and then some. This addiction is a form of self sabotage, psychological reversal, a desire or a compulsion to somehow punish him/herself. This can result from the negative life belief that he/she is a victim, guilty, bad, undeserving or any other of the negative life beliefs listed in Chapter 11. At the same time, I believe they also suffer from a physical condition known as functional hypoadrenia.

Functional hypoadrenia is a condition in which the adrenal glands are in an exhausted state (Hans Selye, M.D.). To get them to function beyond the minimal for survival, the individual must figuratively 'whip' their adrenal glands like a tired horse to make them produce.

The adrenal glands are our 'stress' glands. They produce hormones which allow us to stand and fight, or to rapidly get out of a place when we are in danger. This is the fight or flight mechanism that is so crucial to our survival. We have all heard of the expression, "that gets my adrenalin going" when a person is in a situation that is exciting, whether it is of a positive or negative nature.

Most people are stimulated by controlled danger, such as a roller coaster ride, bungie jumping, parachute jumping, or watching a scary movie. There are many exciting activities that stimulate the adrenals to produce a rush of adrenalin that increases the heart and respiration rate, and prepares the body to produce endorphins which take away our pain. We've all heard of the 'runners high' which runners get from the continuous exercise. This happens because the adrenals produce the hormones that trigger the endorphins.

The chance of winning or losing is also very exciting to a gambler. It brings the adrenalin rush. This is why I believe compulsive gamblers keep coming back, over and over, win or lose. That excitement, combined with a negative life belief for the need for punishment or pain or being guilty, etc., locks in the compulsive gambler.

Compulsive gambling must be treated by balancing the energies in the body by using the procedures of Acu-POWER to conquer the negative life beliefs. Simultaneously, the person must rebuild their adrenal glands with proper nutrition and chiropractic care. Prescribing prednizone or any other steroids will only weaken them more, as the body will be tricked into thinking all is well, and the adrenal glands will produce even less.

For the physical treatment of functional hypoadrenia, in my opinion, there is no one better qualified than a doctor whose practice includes applied kinesiology, most of whom are chiropractic physicians. Restoring the adrenal glands to full function takes time, usually between one to two years.

As mentioned before, the adrenal glands are the stress glands of the body. They respond to four different stresses - physical, chemical, thermal and emotional.

Physical stress is the result of over-tiring the body, not enough sleep, lifting too much, long physical labor, the body and/or spine being out of structural alignment, being injured, trauma of surgery, etc.

Chemical stress means breathing polluted air; drinking unsafe water (or in many communities, tap water containing chlorine), consuming drugs, alcohol, or tobacco; being exposed to pesticides, herbicides, and/or the various poisons and chemicals of the work place; eating 'junk' food (sugar, refined carbohydrates and too much fat), etc.

Taking a trip to the mountains, particularly those like the Rockies where altitudes can get up to 11,000 and 12,000 feet, can cause hypoxyia (a chemical stress of oxygen depletion). For some, just visiting Denver, which is only 5,200 feet, can be very stressful.

Thermal stress is exposing the body to rapid temperature changes when not properly dressed for the change. For example, the service station attendant who doesn't bother to put a coat on to run out for just a couple of minutes to pump gas when it's 25 degrees F (or below) outside; the office worker who does the same to 'run next door' to another building in the winter, the person who works in an air conditioned office in the summer and goes out into the 90 degree street temperature, gets into a closed car that is now 150 degrees in the sun, and then turns on the cold blast of the car air conditioner. Extremes at any temperature for a prolonged period of time, and/or the constant radical changing of temperature, cause stress.

Emotional stress can come from many situations, whether it be family, friends, employees, employers, money problems etc. There is an old story about the man who's wife, girlfriend and car payment were all three months late. That's stress!

Stress is accumulative, and while there may not be a lot in any one category, the accumulation of all the stresses of all the categories mentioned above can quickly add up and have a profound negative effect on the adrenal glands.

It might seem that I am spending a lot of time on the adrenal glands. For the compulsive gambler; however, it is very important that they be treated so that they can respond normally and not have to be 'whipped' to produce.

OBSESSIVE THOUGHTS

"Don't Worry, Be happy" is the name of a popular song in the early '80's. But suppose that you can't stop worrying, that you can't get the worrisome thought out of your mind. This is the plight of millions of people all over the world. Recently, Shari Roan of the Los Angeles Times wrote and article entitled, "Worriers may face real threat." In the article, she quotes Gary Emery, director of the Los Angeles Center of Cognitive Therapy, who states, "Chronic worrying is unrealistic in the sense that it is unhelpful and it's counterproductive." He continues, "It's realistic in a sense that what you're worried about **could** actually happen..." Unfortunately, techniques in the article which were offered to help chronic worriers were aimed at the left brain - the logical brain. The techniques admonished worriers to set aside a specific time of day to worry, say a half hour, and to save all the worrying for then! It sounds logical, but the worrier is illogical! The worrier is emotionally caught up in the process (right brain), and because of imbalance in his/her psychological immune system, is unable to sort out the real from the unreal fears.

Recently, a patient was referred to me who was having obsessive thoughts and worry. She was also seeing an orthodox counselor. After her first twenty minute visit, during which we balanced her energies with Acu-POWER procedures, she reported that in her next counseling session she made more progress than she had ever made before. In her second visit with me we found that most, if not all, of her obsessive thoughts were caused by her feeling of guilt. We treated this and found that she needed a flower remedy to help her center herself.

To treat a person with obsessive thoughts, it is necessary to check for and treat neurological disorganization, then check for and treat all the degrees of psychological reversal. With this type of person it is best to test for all the negative life beliefs and issues first and treat if necessary with the treatment procedures described in those chapters. After this has been done, have the person think of any obsessive thought and then treat them with the basic Acu-POWER treatment described in Chapter 10.

Chapter 24

Testing and Treating Yourself

By this time, you are probably wondering how to test and treat yourself. Often, it is inconvenient or impossible to have someone available to test you.

Callahan was presented with this problem after writing his book, Five Minute Phobia Cure. While he was appearing on various radio talk shows to promote the book, one of his radio hosts asked him if he could treat listeners if they called in. He thought for a while and said that he would try. Knowing that the majority of phobias had an imbalance in the Stomach energy meridian (test point 1, See Figure 8a), he would ask callers to think of their phobia, to quantify it in their own minds and then to tap under the eyes (treatment point one, See Figure 8b). If it did not go down in ten or fifteen seconds, he had them tap the psychological reversal point (See Figures 12 a&b) while saying, "I deeply accept myself even though I am afraid of_____." Then he had them continue tapping under the eyes. If progress stopped again, he would have them go through the brain balancing procedure and or the mini-reversal procedure until all fear was gone, or/until it had gone down at least to a two or three. Occasionally, in resistant cases, he would have the caller tap on treatment point two, the spleen energy meridian (See Figure 8b). That would take care of most of the rest of the phobias. In over one hundred cases, he had a 97% success rate, that is, the callers were able to get down to a '3' or below. Most were able to get to '1' (completely free of the fear).

This procedure may be used for yourself or anyone else but without muscle testing to monitor the progress, it can be much slower.

Callahan did develop a way to self test:

1. Bend over and touch your toes to loosen up. Find out how far you can bend over without bouncing (See Figure 15a).

Figure 15a

If you can't touch your toes, put a pencil, pen, ruler or other measuring object in one of your hands and bend over until it touches the floor (See Figure 15b).

Figure 15b

Note exactly how far it projects beyond your hand while you are bent over without 'bouncing'. This is your measuring point.

2. If you can easily touch your toes and go beyond, stand on a book or a step so you can make an accurate measurement (See Figure 15c).

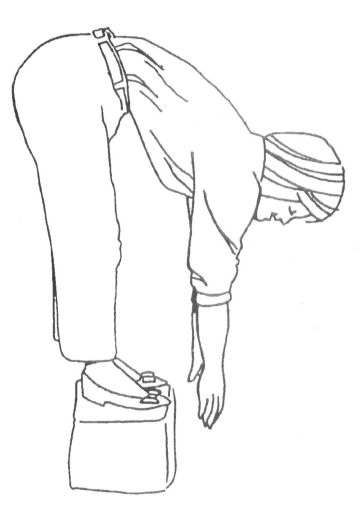

Figure 15c

3. Think of the phobia, issue, etc. and keeping it in mind, bend over again. You will not be able to bend over as far. This is equivalent to someone testing your arm and it becoming weak. The fact that you can not bend over as far indicates that your flexor muscles are now 'weak'. Use this indicator the same as the regular muscle testing.

4. Sometimes there is no difference in how far you can bend over. If this occurs, tap on the psychological reversal point (See Figures 12 a&b) while saying, "I deeply accept myself even though I can't test myself." Repeat the bending over testing procedure, and if there is now a difference, you are ready to proceed.

5. If there still is no difference, tap on the brain balance point and go through the entire sequence (nine steps) while thinking of your inability to test yourself. In most cases this will correct the block and you will be able to test yourself. If you are still not able to notice a difference in the amount you can bend over, have someone else test your strong indicator muscle while you are thinking of testing yourself. Touch each test point (See Figure 8a) in sequence until you find one that abolishes the weakness, and then tap the corresponding treatment points (See Figure 8b) until you can test yourself. There may be several mini-reversals which occur, and these have to be treated when they occur.

6. It may be that you have neurological disorganization as described in Chapter 9. This must be tested by another person and treated.

Occasionally, there are those few individuals who can't be treated for their inability to test themselves. This is still in research as to how it can be overcome.

If you are able to see a difference as to your ability to bend forward, to touch your toes, you are now ready to test. In the case of a phobia, issue, negative life belief, addictions or any other problem, think or make the statement as you have been instructed in those chapters. When weakness is found (you can't bend over as far), repeat the process of bending over, this time with only one arm extended and measure (See Figure 15d).

Figure 15d

Touch the other hand to the test points (See Figure 15e - illustrates touching test point 9), starting with test point one and working your way through until you find the test point that allows you to bend over farther. That is the test point involved. Tap on the corresponding treatment points and proceed as usual.

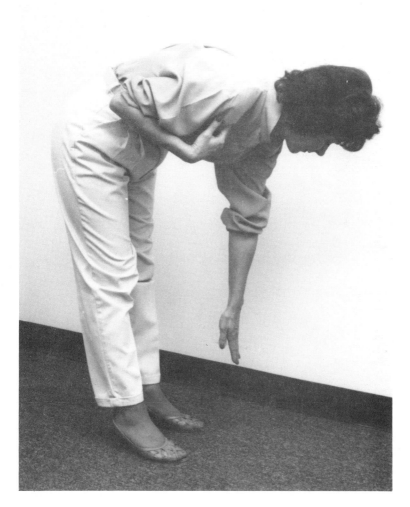

Figure 15e

There is another method of self testing which requires a little more awareness of one's body. Developed by Gerald Deutsch, D.C., his is called the "O" ring muscle test.

Instead of bending over, put the index finger and the thumb of either hand together (See Figure. 16a).

Figure 16a

Then put your opposite index finger in the "O" at the point where the thumb and the index finger of the hand touch. Apply just enough pressure (strength) to the "O" ring hand so you can't pull the index finger of the opposite hand through the juncture of the index finger and thumb (See Figure 16b).

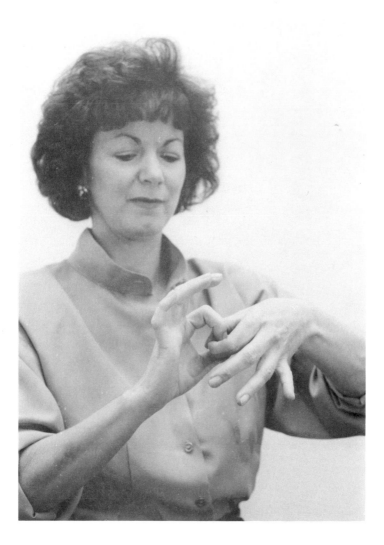

Figure 16b

Think of your phobia or issue or make a false statement, such as stating that your name is something that it is not. There should be a weakening of the "O" ring hand so your opposite index finger pulls through (See Figure 16c). If not, lessen your pressure so that it will barely hold and repeat.

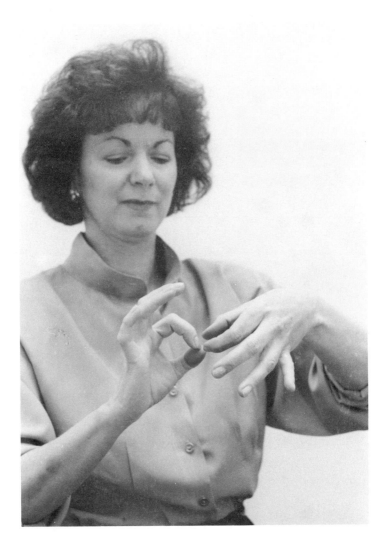

Figure 16c

If you find that you are not able to do this, go through the same treatment procedure as outlined above with the bending over technique until you are able.

This "O" ring testing is far less conspicuous and can be done almost anywhere without attracting attention. It does, however, require a little practice. The "O" ring testing can be done with either hand making the "O" ring, depending which feels more comfortable and natural to you.

To find the test point that is active, simply hold both hands over each point while trying to pull through the "O" ring, until you find a point where it remains strong (See Figure 16d).

Figure 16d

Chapter 25

Problem Cases

From time to time you or someone you are helping will not progress as -expected when using Acu-POWER procedures. Some conditions require the treatment of a psychologist or psychiatrist in addition to Acu-POWER. Individuals in this situation should be referred to a reputable doctor. The combination of the two therapies usually will be successful whereas either one, done individually, will not.

If you find you can not discover any of the test points that will strengthen the indicator muscle when it weakens, those individuals are probably dehydrated and need to drink at least one to two full glasses of water. To test, have the person sip some water and hold it in his/her mouth, repeat your therapy localization testing. If the indicator muscle strengthens on one of the test points, dehydration is the problem. If not, review the location of the test points to determine if the person is touching the correct point. Being just an inch off can make a lot of difference. Be sure that the person understands your directions clearly, such as when you instruct them to touch two inches above the navel or two inches below the navel or just above the pubic bone, etc. Sometimes the point just above the pubic bone is difficult to locate while in a seated position, particularly if the person is overweight.

The mind is very precise, therefore you need to be very precise in the questions you ask or the statements you ask the person to say. Like a computer (but much more complex), the brain will only respond to the right question or statement.

I am reminded of a patient I was treating who had a very difficult problem in a relationship. She had been employed by a person and was also in a very intimate personal relationship with him. She discovered that he was involved in what appeared to be either unethical or illegal business dealings. Even though she was not involved, she could have been indicted by association if the situation went any further. She reported her findings to the business, which stood to possibly lose quite a lot of money. She felt betrayed by his actions and guilty for reporting them.

After treating her, it appeared that she had worked through these feelings. When she thought about it and made a statement that she had released her feelings, her indicator muscle remained strong but she said that it still made her feel uncomfortable. The body doesn't lie, but it appeared that in this case it had. This was a case of not asking the right question. I then asked her to say, "I am *not* deceiving myself when I say that I am over this problem with_____." Her indicator muscle immediately weakened.

If, after treating a problem, you find the indicator muscle stays strong, signifying the problem has been eliminated, but the person still has uncomfortable feelings, have the person make the statement, "I am not deceiving myself about this problem." If the statement is false, the indicator muscle will weaken.

In some instances the left brain (logical) will not communicate with the right brain and answer the question in a logical manner. After all, it is logical that getting over a problem will be good for the person.

Continuing with the story of my patient, I then asked her to think about the problem with her emotional brain -- her right brain. Her indicator muscle weakened. I then asked her to think about the problem with her left brain -- her logical brain; the indicator muscle remained strong! This indicated that the right and left brain were not communicating.

Treating the regular Brain Balance point on the back of the hand was unsuccessful in her case. I then asked her to continue to think about the problem with her *right (emotional) brain* while she therapy localized (touched) the various test points until she found one that would abolish the weakness. She then was instructed to tap those corresponding treatment points (rather than the usual Brain Balance point on the back of the hand) while going through the Brain Balance procedure (See Chapter 10).

During the procedure, when she got down to a '5' she mentioned that she felt herself becoming very angry and *refused* to allow herself to go any lower. I then had her say, "I will *allow* myself to *overcome my refusal* to get lower than a '5' on this problem," and her indicator muscle weakened.

Repeating the affirmation, "I deeply accept myself even though I *refuse to allow* myself to get below a '5' on this problem." while tapping the regular psychological reversal treatment point was not successful. I then had her therapy localize the other test points until she found one which abolished the weakness, and I had her tap those points while repeating the above affirmation. In most cases this will resolve the reversal problem as it did for her.

If the person continues to become reversed, or is unsuccessful in overcoming the reversal, it will probably be necessary to give him/her Bach Rescue Remedy, MinTran or Min-Ball. See Chapter 9 for sources.

Often what seems to be a single phobia has many facets. For instance, fear of flying can be broken down into several different fears such as claustrophobia, fear of loss of control, fear of hitting something while taxiing out to the runway, fear of take off, fear of the climb, fear of heights, fear of turbulence, fear of not being able to see out in the clouds, fear of the descent, fear of the landing, and/or fear of the mechanical condition of the airplane. Each one of these may have to be treated separately.

Individuals who are afraid of elevators often experience claustrophobia, fear of loss of control, fear of the space below or above the elevator, fear of getting stuck between floors, etc. Again, each has to be treated individually.

Callahan, in his book Five Minute Phobia Cure, describes four false beliefs or fallacies that may impede or prevent successful treatment.

First, some individuals and even therapists believe that there are underlying causes beneath all phobias, that phobias were "masking devices" and therefore, if the phobia is cured, another one will replace it.

Second, some people believe fear is desirable because it creates character. They believe that if a person is fearful in certain situations it gives him/her depth, therefore, fear is "good".

The third fallacy described in Callahan's book is that phobias make people creative. In truth, however, they don't.

All writers, composers and artists at one time or another have stared at a blank piece of paper or empty canvas, so fearful, that they were unable to begin.

The fourth fallacy is that phobias give people the competitive edge. Individuals who believe this are not able to distinguish fear from excitement. Excitement provides an adrenalin rush that gives the athlete or actor the vitality to perform to the best of his/her ability. Fear, on the other hand, can cause the actor to miss lines or the athlete to hold back.

These four points are myths. If you or someone whom you are treating thinks they are true, reassure yourself or that person they are not. It may be necessary to treat for reversal to eliminate them.

Postscript

Goodheart states, "The body is simply intricate and intricately simple." For instance, the simple act of picking up a cup and bringing it to your mouth to drink requires millions of nerve impulses, perfect coordination of numerous muscles, and countless chemical reactions.

The same is true of our mind in its emotional and psychological functioning. Thought processes not only affect the emotions, but the emotions affect the production of hormones, which affect the function of all organs and systems of the body.

As you have read in this book, there are many different emotions of varying degrees which, if not in proper proportion, can make our lives miserable and interfere with our survival.

There are numerous ways to alter these emotions chemically, but most have unwanted side effects with the exception of nutritional and flower remedies. The various counseling types of treatment and hypnosis usually take long periods of time and in many cases are very emotionally painful. Acu-POWER procedures are non-invasive, rapid and long lasting, most times resulting in permanent corrections.

Most individuals can see the vast applications of Acu-POWER procedures in everything we do in our lives. The applications in counseling, education, sales, sports, business, training programs and wellness programs are as numerous as one can imagine.

To some, however, this procedure may seem too simple to be as powerful as it is when properly applied. Again quoting Goodheart, for those that can look with eyes that see, listen with ears that hear and touch with hands that feel, great things are possible.

It is my hope that you, whether lay person or professional, can use and improve on the Acu-POWER procedures so that phobias, anxieties, addictions, love pain, rejection, post traumatic stress syndrome, compulsive behavior, and self limiting and self destructive negative life beliefs will no longer rule your life or the lives of your loved ones or individuals you treat.

* * *

For information on audio and video cassettes or to be included on a mailing list to receive information on new Acu-POWER treatment procedures as they become available, write to Dr. James V. Durlacher, P.O. Box 27724, Tempe, AZ 85285. Tel.(602) 890-8767

About the Author

Dr. James V. Durlacher began practicing applied kinesiology in 1964, the same year it was discovered. He is a 1963 Magna Cum Laude graduate of the Palmer College of Chiropractic and was a faculty member for several years.

He has written numerous papers which have been published in national chiropractic journals, and in the Proceedings of the International College of Applied Kinesiology of which he is a Charter Teaching Diplomate.

He has been featured on numerous television and radio talk shows speaking on and demonstrating the procedures of this book. In addition, he has taught over 2,500 hours of basic and advanced applied kinesiology courses around the nation.

Dr. Durlacher continues to practice at 448 E. Southern, Tempe, AZ 85282

Testimonials

Claustrophobia

I'm a four feet eight adult woman and as far back as I can remember I have always had an *overwhelming fear* of getting on an crowded elevator or being in any crowd. In any crowded situation I would have a feeling of being smothered and would start to shake, my hands would get cold and sweaty, my heart would feel like it was going to explode, my face would lose all its color and on top of this I would have to try to control my overwhelming need to scream, "let me out"! I never went anywhere that would require the use of an elevator. In another instance I remember a terrifying incident at a carnival when I was going to take two of my boys on a ride in which three were seated abreast. I was in the middle. As soon as the three of us were in the seat and secured, I felt overwhelmed by fear and started yelling to be let out. While I was immediately released, I needed assistance to even get out of the seat because I felt so weak and was crying uncontrollably. Since I wouldn't let my boys ride alone, their day was spoiled.

Through Acu-POWER treatment I have been completely cured of this terrible fear. Just in time too. Soon after being treated I started to work for a junior high school with their Trainable Mentally Handicapped class. Part of my job was to take these students out into the community to teach them self-reliance. One day we went to the mall where it was necessary to show the students how to use the elevator. After all eight children (one in a wheelchair), a teacher and two assistants filed on

the elevator, it was my turn. At first I was tempted to tell them
that I would meet them upstairs but decided to give the elevator
a try. Even though it was so crowded that I couldn't turn
around and everyone towered over me so that I couldn't see
over anyone, I felt calm and relaxed where previously I would
have been in a panic. This time there were no sweaty palms, no
rapid heart beat, no desire to scream, "Let me out!", just the
greatest feeling that I was able to ride the crowded elevator and
enjoy it!

Melanie Patton
Chandler, AZ

Addiction-Bitterness-Grief

I used to have a very strong addiction to sweets but
thanks to Acu-POWER I no longer have a compulsion to eat
them.

For many years I was unable to converse with my step-
son, who is an alcoholic, without feeling bitter because of his
mistreatment of both his father and myself. When he would call
I would never talk to him but immediately hand the phone to his
father. If his father was not at home I would tell him so and
hang up. After Acu-POWER treatment he called when his father was out and I actually had a pleasant conversation with
him. It wasn't until after I hung up that I realized that I had
changed my attitude toward him. I had allowed myself to look
at him in a different light. It was also wonderful not to be
shaking as I always was before.

Twenty years ago my son was blinded as a result of an
automobile accident. Every time he came to visit I would relive
the traumatic memory and be crying or on the verge of tears the
whole time he was home. After Acu-POWER treatment, for the
first time since the accident, I have been able to look at my son
without heartbreak and actually enjoy his visit. I was euphoric!

It has helped me to accept his blindness and release my grief and pity. I feel so free!

Margaux L. Furrer
Tempe, AZ

Sexual Molestion-Anger

My two oldest boys, ages 9 and 10 were sexually molested by an adult male relative. Both my wife and myself were so angry that we were not rational. I was so irrational that I would have ended up in jail if I had followed up on the thoughts I had.

A period of six months had elapsed before we became aware of the molestation and we started in counseling immediately. My wife mentioned the situation to Dr. Durlacher and he offered to help using his Acu-POWER treatment. We were skeptical at first but allowed him to see the boys.

After about a 15 minute session the boys appeared to be completely free of this very traumatic emotional experience. In later conversation with them we found that it was true.

He then treated myself and my wife for our anger and we too were able to release all the pent-up anger and bitterness which had been consuming us and go on with our lives.

I must share another experience concerning my wife. She had always been very scared of heights, particularly while driving in the mountains with cliffs dropping off hundreds of feet at the edge of the road. When she had to drive to our summer place in the mountains she used to get almost frantic with fear. After one 10 minute Acu-POWER treatment all the fear was gone and now she actually enjoys her drives in the mountains!

Paul T.
Mesa, AZ

Addiction to Chocolate

I had a compulsion to eat chocolate anytime I was under stress. Using the procedure on the Acu-POWER tapes I was able to stop eating chocolate.

Diana Rosser
Mesa, AZ

Stopped Smoking

As a flight attendant I was a wreck on my flights, not being able to smoke, but using the Acu-POWER tapes I was able to stop smoking and now I am calm and relaxed.

Holly, Flight Attendant
Tempe, AZ

Fear of Water

My wife was a hydrophobic when it came to the possibility of getting her head under water in the pool or anywhere for that matter. In fact she would become frantic if she got near the deeper parts of the pool.

In just 12 minutes, Acu-POWER treatment completely cured her phobia. I was even more impressed because she does not understand English and I had to act as an interpreter relaying the instructions of what to do.

Gabe
Mesa, AZ

Fear of Heights

I was afraid to stay on any floor above the third in a building. I was also very nervous while flying. Interstate highway and freeway driving was very difficult, particularly if I got behind a large truck. After one hour of Acu-POWER treatment I am now completely relaxed while traveling by car or plane and can sleep in a room that is above the third floor.

David
Phoenix, AZ

Guilt-Grief

My guilt and grief had been eating away at me for 27 years since my son was killed in an automobile accident in which I was the driver. I walked away from it shaken but uninjured.

I had been in counseling many times before without significant help. In about fifteen minutes of the Acu-POWER treatment I was able to finally accept the death of my son, forgive myself and release all the guilt and grief that I have suffered all those years. I hope that anyone who reads this will use the Acu-POWER procedures to find the peace of mind for themselves as I have.

Florence C. Porter
Tempe, AZ

Rejection

While I was receiving chiropractic adjustments by you in your office, you sensed my emotional distress and tactfully asked if I wanted to find out what was causing it. After some testing, I found, much to my surprise, that I felt I was undeserving. You had me tap on the side of my hand while reading the deserving affirmation (see Chapter 11) and I began crying uncontrollably while reading the first line. The rejection I had experienced in my life was so severe that it took several appointments before I could read the full affirmation comfortably. Thanks to your patience and Acu-POWER I was able to overcome my emotional wounds.

Lois Swanson
Sun City West, AZ

Fear of Freeway Driving

I was raised in a small midwestern town with many dirt roads so the thoughts of driving the California freeways terrified me. Acu-POWER has changed my life. It has been integral in breaking through fears and traumas and has strengthened me at all levels. I highly recommend Acu-POWER to anyone seeking increased self-mastery.

Patricia A. Mindorff
Los Angeles, CA

Fear of Spiders-Eating Disorder

Your simple, yet extremely effective program for the treatment of phobias has had a profound effect on the lives of my wife and myself. Her fear of spiders and my own eating disorder were problems which we simply lived with for many years. After only a couple of visits with you at your office the situations reversed themselves almost overnight. My wife, Tracey and I will never have to face these previously difficult problems again.

Russ Mathieu
New Haven, CT

Life Transformed

Several years ago Dr. Durlacher actually saved my life by using Acu-POWER, ridding me of a deep-seated phobia which had pushed into a dangerous state of depression and driven me to a depth with suicidal intentions. Today, my life has truly been transformed. I am now a very contented, happy and peaceful   person, thanks to Dr. Durlacher and Acu-POWER.

Charlotte K. Gussie-Richmond
Mesa, AZ

What Professionals Are Saying

I had been introduced to Acu-POWER treatment program recently. Here are summaries of two case histories that would have taken much more time to treat with procedures I would have normally used.

The case of R.S.: R.S. originally started therapy in 1992, and attended sessions for approximately one year. At that time she was not in a serious romantic relationship. During the course of therapy she met a man who was very different in background and life direction. She stated she was very attracted to him, and began to date. She left treatment reporting she felt centered and content and was thinking about a more serious level of involvement with her friend.

In June of 1994 R.S. resumed therapy. At the first session she appeared quite distressed. She had married her friend; however, the relationship had deteriorated due to his drug use, financial manipulation of her funds and other behavioral patterns which are often part and parcel of substance abuse. He was in a residential treatment facility at this time. Many issues were vying for attention - her desire to have children, the fear this would not happen, and feelings that her present situation was not amicable to undertaking such a task. This issue was causing her great stress. R.S. felt that not being a mother would signify a failure in her life. She indicated working on this problem was timely and agreed to begin with the new approach of Acu-POWER to address her distress.

She was able to rapidly release all her fear during that session.

On her next visit, one week later, she stated that none of the fear had returned; however, on the third visit she said that she was beginning to feel apprehension concerning not achieving motherhood. The Acu-POWER treatment was repeated and the apprehension quickly disappeared. R.S. recognized there were many issues surrounding her marriage that she felt uncomfortable with and that she still had time to consider a family at some future time.

As of August 19, 1994 she continued to be free of her feelings of fear concerning not having children.

The case of M.A.: M.A. is a highly educated, motivated, intelligent woman in her early forties. She has worked in the field of music education for many years and enjoys a highly respected reputation. Her altruism and sincerity to offer her students broad learning opportunities was readily apparent.

M.A. accepted a position in a parochial school teaching various grade levels. In addition to the usual hours of classroom teaching and its' preparation she was also expected to supervise playground activities and participate in weekend religious services even though she was not a member of that denomination.

Eventually, some rather unfortunate political situations within the institution became evident. This involved lack of administrative support for teacher, undue influence of parents and resulting negative attitudes by many members of the staff.

At one point M.A. overheard the conversation of a cafeteria worker indication to another employee that replacing her would be beneficial to the school. Reporting that this was painful to hear, she stated that she felt angered that someone with little or no understanding of what her job entailed would speak with such a judgmental attitude. She also believed the worker was aware she was within earshot and would overhear what was said.

M.A. reported to me that her indignation was interfering with her ability to achieve the emotional stability necessary to perform her job. She was treated with Acu-POWER procedures and was completely free of all anger in just 15 minutes in that single session in May, 1994. M.A. was checked periodically over the next four months and as of August, 1994 she reported no recurring negative feelings or thoughts concerning the situation.

Anger can be a difficult emotion for clients to process and release. It often takes a great deal of time to treat and even then not always successfully by traditional therapies. I consider this case a prime example of the effectiveness of Acu-POWER.

Linda Goodman-Bone, Psychotherapist
Mesa, AZ

Using the Acu-POWER procedures has been a great addition to my toolbox. The immediate results of feeling calm were especially appreciated and made quick believers of a few psychotherapists who also happen to be my patients."

Paul J. Loch, D.C.
Exter, NH

I have been using the Acu-POWER treatment with my clients and the results have been remarkable!

Here are some examples:

Client #1: This woman has had a life-long sugar/chocolate addiction and in one session, she no longer has any desire for sweets. I had her husband take her to a bakery after the session just to see what her reaction would be. She called me later that evening and told me that they went to two bakeries, not one. And, she had absolutely no desire for anything at either bakery. It has been over a week now and she called today that she has not had any desire for one drop of sugar. She told me that not only has it been effortless for her not to eat any sugar or chocolate but that she feels more relaxed in general than she has in years.

Client #2: Has had a fear of flying since 1989 when she was taking a trip and the plane had to make an emergency landing. She is scheduled to fly to Michigan in 2 weeks. She was so afraid that she wouldn't be able to actually take the flight, she also made a train reservation. At the end of the session, she said, "It's gone! It's gone out of my body! I can tell the fear is no longer there. I feel like jumping and shouting!" (Which I encouraged her to do).

Client #3: Is a 6 year old boy who has had a terrible fear of going upstairs, outside, or into his room alone. He refuses to go into his room alone because of "the monster that's hiding under my bed." After one session, his mother called me the next morning and said, "I have really good news." She reported that her son crawled in bed with her and her husband during the night, which is a common occurrence. Then, at about 6:45 a.m., she asked him to go up to his bedroom and get some clothes for school. When he returned downstairs, she said to him, "Honey, isn't it wonderful that you weren't afraid to go upstairs and into your room alone? He replied, "I wasn't scared at all and I didn't even turn on the light in my bedroom!"

Client #4: Has been a group facilitator for many years, however, she still suffers from a fear of public speaking. After one session, she called a couple of days later to report that her group facilitation the night before went fabulously. She said, "I felt lighter in my body and I was a lot more spontaneous than ever before. I just had a great time! This process is incredible. My whole body felt totally different."

Client #5: Has had a fear of cancer for many years because both of his parents died of it. At the end of the session, he said he felt totally relaxed in his abdominal area, which is the place he usually holds tension. He stated it was really difficult to think about the fear anymore.

Client #6: Had gone to her dentist's office for a routine cleaning. After about 5 minutes in the chair she heard a female scream and saw the receptionist/hygienist being hit on the head with a hammer. The attacker turned out to be the receptionist's estranged husband. He shouted, "If I can't see my daughter again, neither will you." He had killed her. She did not sleep that night, terrified that since she had witnessed the murder and he looked directly at her, he would come and kill her too even though he was arrested and was in jail. She contacted me and I treated her with Acu-POWER and in one session, she was able to completely release this terror and has been able to sleep peacefully ever since.

Shellie Stoffer, Human Development Consultant
Santa Cruz, CA

I have been using Acu-POWER techniques in my practice for the past nine years with fantastic results. I have seen the lives of my patients dramatically changed as a result of these techniques. As a teacher of applied kinesiology I can tell you that Dr. Durlacher has done an excellent job of organizing information from a variety of sources for presentation in a very readable format. This book can change your life. It can change the lives of your friends and loved ones. I highly recommend this book!

James D.W. Hogg, D.C.
Rock Island, IL

I have been using Acu-POWER over the past five years with much success clinically as well as personally. Areas of fears, phobias and compulsive behavior like eating and smoking are most efficiently handled. The simplicity of Acu-POWER allows easy access into even the busiest practices. So I must say the beauty of Acu-POWER is not only its efficiency, but also its simplicity of application.

P. Anthony Paolucci, D.C.
Maryville, IL

A famous proverb states, "Give a man a fish, feed him for a day; teach him how to fish, feed him for a lifetime. The information in this book will teach you how to solve many of your internal problems on your own -- For a Lifetime!

Christopher P. Neck, Ph.D.
Department of Management
Virginia Technical University
Blacksburg, VA

As a practicing chiropractic physician and a mental health counselor with doctorates in chiropractic and health psychology and behavioral medicine, I know the importance of having effective clinical procedures in the management of such conditions as phobias, addictions, and post traumatic stress responses. I am pleased to report that Dr. Durlacher has done just that. I can also attest that his procedures are simple but astoundingly effective, having utilized them in my practice.

Dr. Durlacher has written an impressive text that is lucid, simple and orderly. It not only reflects his erudition and originality but his charm and his persuasiveness as a teacher of applied kinesiology.

In Freedom From Fear Forever, Dr. Durlacher explains vividly his techniques of Acu-POWER. The chapter on psychological reversal alone is worth the price of the book. This book belongs not only in the hands of those who hurt emotionally, but in the libraries of those health professionals who treat such patients. This book will no doubt be a resounding success for many individuals who turn to self help books. Hopefully it will extend its reach far and beyond that population!

Edward C. Sullivan, D.C., Ph.D.,Vice President,
Council on Behavioral Health of the American Chiropractic
Association.
Mt.Vernon, WA

A month after you found the emotional cause of my neck and back pain and your Acu-Power treatment I am still free of the years of pain.

In addition I am now free from what I call an "ancy" feeling that I had in the evening after things got quiet. Something kept gnawing in my solar plexus and to attempt to relieve the gnawing I would get something to nibble on. There were times I felt I wanted something, but didn't know what and I would go the refrigerator, open the door, look and then close the door without removing anything. Even after I nibbled the "ancy" feeling didn't go away. Thanks to the acu-Power treatment, I can now lie down in the evening and feel relaxed and comfortable.

I have found your book <u>Freedom From Fear Forever</u> of great interest and full of invaluable information in assisting me in working with my clients.

This is a self-help book that really can help and make a difference for anyone who reads it.

Evelyn Budd-Michaels, Ph. D.
Reseda, CA

<u>Freedom from Fear Forever</u> is informative and exciting. It is a superb text for any health care provider. Anyone who utilizes applied kinesiology, acupuncture or acupressure in their practices should have it in their library.

James A. Revels, Jr., D.C.
Columbia, SC

An excellent volume. Dr. Durlacher has taken the best of his experience under applied kinesiology and Dr. Callahan's work and produced a book of great value to all the healing arts as well as solid hope for disturbed patients.

George J. Goodheart, D.C.
Discoverer and Developer   of Applied Kinesiology
Grosse Pointe Woods, MI

Recommended Reading

Addict, A Doctors Odyssy, James Dewitt, M.D.

Ageless Body, Timeless Mind, Deepak Chopra, M.D.

Awaken The Giant Within, Anthony Robbins

Chicken Soup For the Soul, Mark Victor Hansen & Jack Canfield

Dear Doc..., John Pursch, M.D.

Eat More, Weigh Less, Dean Ornish, M.D.

Everyone Is An Athlete, Philip Maffetone, D.C.

Five Minute Phobia Cure, Roger J. Callahan. Ph.D.

Healing And The Mind, Bill Moyers

Heal Thyself, The Bach Flower Remedies, Edward Bach

How Executives Overcome Their Fear Of Public Speaking and Other Phobias, Roger J. Callahan, Ph.D.

Perfect Health, Deepak Chopra, M.D.

Psychodietetics, Emanual Cheraskin, M.D.

Pulling Your Own Strings, Wayne W. Dyer, Ph.D.

Quantum Healing, Deepak Chopra, M.D.

Real Magic, Wayne W. Dyer, Ph.D.

The Man Who Tapped The Secrets Of The Universe, Glenn Clark

Vibrational Medicine, Richard Gerber, M.D.

Why Do I Eat When I'm Not Hungry?, Roger J. Callahan, Ph.D.

You'll Be Better, George Goodheart, D.C.

Your Body Dosen't Lie, John Diamond, M.D.

Your Erroneous Zones, Wayne W. Dyer, Ph.D.

References

Callahan, Roger, A Rapid Treatment for Phobias and Psychological Reversal, Collected Papers of the International College of Applied Kinesiology, Lawrence KS, 1981

Callahan, Roger, Five Minute Phobia Cure, Enterprise Publishing, Inc. Wilmington, DE, 1985

Chopra, Deepak, Quantum Healing, Bantam Books, New York, NY, 1989

Deutsch, Gerald, Personal conversations, Tempe, AZ, 1993

DuPont, Robert, Phobia: A Comprehensive Summery of Modern Treatments, Brunner/Mazel, New York, NY 1982

Gerber, Richard, Vibrational Medicine, Bear & Co., Santa Fe, NM, 1988

Goodheart, George, International College of Applied Kinesiology, Workshop Manuals Privately Published, Detroit, MI, 1965-1989

Goodwin, Donald W., Is Alcoholism Hereditary? Ballantine Publishing, New York, NY, 1976

Jeffers, Susan, Feel The Fear And Do It Anyway, Fawcett Columbine, New York, 1987

Kadushin, Charles and Boulanger, Ghislaine, The Vietman Veteran Redifined, Fact & Fiction, Lawrence Erlbaum Associates, Publishers, Hillside, NJ 1986

Moyers, Bill, Healing And The Mind, Doubleday, New York, NY, 1993

Ornish, Dean, Eat More and Weigh Less, Harper Collins Publishers, New York, 1993

Palmer, D. D., The Chiropractic Adjuster, 1911, Reprint, Palmer College Of Chiropractic Press, Davenport,   IA, 1962

Pursch, John, Dear Doc..., CompCare Publications, Minneapolis, MN, 1985

Robbins, Anthony, Awaken The Giant Within. Simon & Schuster, New York, 1991

Walther, David S., Applied Kinesiology Synopsis, Systems DC, Pueblo, CO, 1988

Appendix

COMMON AND UNUSUAL PHOBIAS

Fear of: **Scientific Name**

Air ....Aerophobia
Animals ....Zoophobia
Auroral lights ....Auroraphobia
Bacteria ....Bacteriophobia
Beards ....Pogonophobia
Bees...Apiphobia
Being afraid ....Phobophobia
Being alone..............................Autophobia
Being beaten............................Rhabdophobia
Being bound.............................Merinthophobia
Being buried alive.....................Taphophobia
Being dirty................................Automysophobia
Being egotistical.......................Autophobia
Being scratched........................Amychophobia
Being stared at.........................Scopophobia
Birds..Ornithophobia
Blood ....Hematophobia
Blushing...................................Ereuthophobia
Books.......................................Bibliophobia
Cancer.....................................Cancerophobia
Cats ....Ailurophobia
Certain name............................Onomatophobia
Chickens ....Alektorophobia
Childbirth..................................Tocophobia

Children.....................................Pediophobia
China ....Sinophobia
Choking.....................................Pnigophobia
Cholera.....................................Cholerophobia
Churches...................................Ecclesiaphobia
Clouds......................................Nephophobia
Cold...Psychrophobia
Colors ....Chromatophobia
Confinement...............................Claustrophobia
Corpse......................................Necrophobia
Crossing a bridge ....Gephyrophobia
Crowds.....................................Ochlophobia
Crystals ....Crystallophobia
Dampness..................................Hygrophobia
Darkness ....Achluophobia
Dawn ....Eosophobia
Daylight.....................................Phengophobia
Death ....Necrophobia
Deformity...................................Dysmorphophobia
Demons, devils ....Demonophobia
Depth ....Bathophobia
Dirt ....Mysophobia
Diesease....................................Nosophobia
Disorder.....................................Ataxiophobia
Dogs ....Cynophobia
Dolls...Pediophobia
Draught ....Anemophobia
Dreams ....Oneirphobia
Drink ....Potophobia
Drinking ....Dipsophobia
Drugs..Pharmacophobia
Duration ....Chronophobia
Dust..Amathophobia
Electricity...................................Electrophobia
Elevated places ....Acrophobia
Empty rooms...............................Kenophobia
Enclosed space............................Claustrophobia
England & English.......................Anglophobia
Everything..................................Panophobia
Eyes..Ommatophobia
Feces...Coprophobia
Failure.......................................Kakorraphiaphobia

Fatigue ....Ponophobia
Feathers ....Pteronophobia
Fire ....Pyrophobia
Fish ....Ichthyophobia
Flashes ....Selaphobia
Flogging ....Mastigophobia
Flood ....Antlophobia
Flowers ....Anthophobia
Flute ....Aulophobia
Flying ....Aerophobia
Fog...Homicholophobia
Food ....Sitophobia
Foreigners ....Zenophobia
France & French things ....Gallophobia
Freedom..................................Eleutherophobia
Fur ....Doraphobia
Gaiety ....Cherophobia
Germany ....Germanophobia
Germs ....Spermophobia
Ghosts ....Phasmophobia
Glass......................................Crystallophobia
God ....Theophobia
Going to bed ....Clinophobia
Grave......................................Taphophobia
Gravity ....Barophobia
Hair.......................................Chaetophobia
Heart disease ....Cardiophobia
Heat.......................................Thermophobia
Heaven ....Ouranophobia
Heights...................................Acrophobia
Heredity..................................Patroiophobia
Home surroundings ....Ecophobia
Home ....Domatophobia
Horses....................................Hippophobia
Human beings...........................Anthropophobia
Ice, frost ....Cryophobia
Ideas ....Ideophobia
Illness.....................................Nosemaphobia
Imperfection............................Atelophobia
Infection..................................Mysophobia
Infinity ....Apeirophobia
Inoculation..............................Trypanophobia

Insanity.................................Lyssophobia
Insects.................................Entomophobia
Itching.................................Acarophobia
Jealousy...............................Zelophobia
Justice.................................Dikephobia
Knees..................................Genuphobia
Lakes..................................Limnophobia
Leprosy...............................Leprophobia
Lice....................................Pediculophobia
Light...................................Photophobia
Lightning.............................Astrapophobia
Machinery............................Mechanophobia
False statements....................Mythophobia
Many things..........................Polyphobia
Marriage..............................Gamophobia
Meat...................................Carnophobia
Men....................................Androphobia
Metals.................................Metallophobia
Meteors...............................Meteorophobia
Mice...................................Musophobia
Microbes..............................Bacilliphobia
Mind...................................Psychophobia
Mirrors................................Eisoptrophobia
Missiles...............................Ballistophobia
Moisture..............................Hygrophobia
Money.................................Chrometophobia
Monstrosities.........................Teratophobia
Motion................................Kinesophobia
Nakedness............................Gymnophobia
Names.................................Nomatophobia
Needles & pins.......................Belonophobia
Neglect of duty......................Paralipophobia
Negroes...............................Negrophobia
Narrowness...........................Anginaphobia
New....................................Neophobia
Night..................................Nyctophobia
Loud noise............................Phonophobia
Novelty................................Cainophobia
Odors..................................Osmophobia
Odors (body).........................Osphresiophobia
Oneself...............................Autophobia
One thing.............................Monophobia

Open spaces ....Agoraphobia
Pain ....Algophobia
Parasites.................................Parasitophobia
Physical love ....Erotophobia
Places....................................Topophobia
Pleasure ....Hedonophobia
Points....................................Aichurophobia
Poison ....Toxiphobia
Poverty ....Peniaphobia
Pregnancy...............................Maieusiophobia
Precipices...............................Cremnophobia
Punishment ....Poionephobia
Rabies ....Lyssophobia
Railway ....Siderodromophobia
Rain.......................................Ombrophobia
Responsibility..........................Hypegiaphobia
Reptiles..................................Batrachophobia
Ridicule ....Katagelophobia
Rivers ....Potamophobia
Robbers ....Harpaxophobia
Ruin.......................................Atephobia
Russia & Russian......................Russophobia
Rust.......................................Iophobia
Sacred things...........................Hierophobia
Satan.....................................Satanophobia
School ....Scholionophobia
Sea ....Thalassophobia
Sea swell................................Cymophobia
Sex ....Genophobia
Sexual intercourse.....................Coitophobia
Shadows.................................Sciophobia
Sharp objects ....Belonophobia
Shock ....Hormephobia
Sinning ....Peccatophobia
Skin.......................................Dermatophobia
Skin diseases ....Dermatosiophobia
Sitting idle..............................Thaasophobia
Skin of animals ....Doraphobia
Sleep.....................................Hypnophobia
Slime.....................................Blennophobia
Smell.....................................Olfactophobia
Smothering ....Pnigerophobia

Snakes ....Ophidiophobia
Snow.......................................Chionophobia
Society ....Anthropophobia
Solitude ....Eremophobia
Sound......................................Akousticophobia
Sourness ....Acerophobia
Speaking ....Halophobia
Speaking aloud ....Phonophobia
Speech.....................................Lalophobia
Speed ....Tachophobia
Spiders ....Arachnophobia
Spirits ....Demonophobia
Standing upright........................Stasiphobia
Stars ....Siderophobia
Stealing...................................Cleptophobia
Stillness ....Eremophobia
Stings ....Cnidophobia
Stooping...................................Kyphophobia
Strangers ....Xenophobia
String ....Linonophobia
Sun..Heliophobia
Surgical operations.....................Ergasiophobia
Swallowing ....Phagophobia
Syphilis...................................Syphilophobia
Taste......................................Geumatophobia
Teeth......................................Odontophobia
Thirteen at table ....Triskaidekaphobia
Thunder ....Keraunophobia
Being touched............................Haphephobia
Travel ....Hodophobia
Trees......................................Dendrophobia
Trembling ....Tremophobia
Tuberculosis...............................Phthisiophobia
Uncovering the body ....Gymnophobia
Vehicles...................................Amaxophobia
Veneral disease ....Cypridophobia
Void ....Kenophobia
Vomiting...................................Emetophobia
Walking...................................Basiphobia
Wasps ....Spheksophobia
Water ....Hydrophobia
Weakness ....Asthenophobia

Wind......................................Anemophobia
Women...................................Gynophobia
Words ....Logophobia
Work ....Ergasiophobia
Worms ....Helminthophobia
Wounds, injury ....Traumatophobia
Writing..................................Graphophobia
Young girls.............................Parthenophobia

Index

Order Form

Telephone Orders: Call Toll Free 1(800) 529-8836. Have your Visa, MasterCard, Discover or AMEX ready.

Fax Orders: 1 (602) 890-2182

Postal Orders: Van Ness Publishing, P.O. Box 27724, Tempe, AZ 85285-7724

Please send___copy(s) of *Freedom From Fear Forever*, hardcover .... @ $22.95 ea.

Please send___copy(s) of *Freedom From Fear Forever*, softcover .... @ $18.95 ea

Please send___set(s) of *Conquer Your Addictive Urge* audio tapes .... @ $29.95 ea.

Please send___set(s) of *The Rapid Treatment of Phobias and Addictions to Food, Tobacco, Alcohol & Drugs Seminar* Video tapes (Four hours) .... @ $99.95

Ship To:

Name _____

Street _____

City_____State_____Zip _____

Sales Tax: Please add 6.75% for books and tapes shipped to Arizona addresses.

Shipping & Handling:

Book Rate: $2.50 for first book or tape set & $1.00 for each additional book or tape set combination.

Priority Mail: $4.50 for first book or tape set & $1.50 for each additional book or tape set combination.

Payment: Check__ Visa__ M / Card__ Discover__ AMEX__

Card Number:_____Exp.Date____/___

Name on Card_____

Signature_____

Call 800-529-8836 and order now